STAR
WARS IN A
NUCLEAR
WORLD

ALSO AVAILABLE IN VINTAGE SPECIALS

STAR WARS IN A NUCLEAR WORLD

Lord Zuckerman

OM, KCB, FRS

VINTAGE BOOKS
A DIVISION OF RANDOM HOUSE
NEW YORK

First Vintage Books Edition, October 1987

Library of Congress Cataloging-in-Publication Data
Zuckerman, Solly Zuckerman, Lord, 1904–
    Star Wars in a nuclear world.
    Includes index.
    1. Strategic Defense Initiative.   2. Nuclear
weapons.   3. Arms race—History—20th century.
I. Title.
UG743.Z82   1987   358'.1754   87-40001
ISBN 0-394-75445-X (pbk.)

Text design by Julie Duquet

Manufactured in the United States of America
10 9 8 7 6 5 4 3 2 1

CONTENTS

Preface

This short book deals with the nuclear arms-race and President Reagan's Strategic Defense Initiative (SDI) as they relate to the responsibilities of politicians, the military, and scientists. I was invited to address myself to these issues in the E.A. Lane Lecture, given at Clare College, Cambridge, in October 1983 (Chapter Three), and in the Keith Morden Lectures, which I delivered at Portland State University in Oregon in October of 1985 (Chapters One and Two). So as to link the three lectures, some passages in the texts as they were delivered have been interchanged. Some have been brought up to date, while those sections of my Morden lectures, in which I discussed the SDI, have been deleted since this is now the sole topic of Chapter Four, which is an essay-review on SDI that appeared in the 30 January 1986 issue of *The New York Review of Books*. I have not attempted to disguise the fact that the first three chapters are based on texts of lectures, which in some places reflect ideas that I developed in earlier writings, particularly in *Beyond the Ivory Tower*, published in 1970 and now out of print, and in *Nuclear Illusion and Reality*, which appeared in 1982.

In the second part of the book are reprinted a series of interrelated articles which complement the four chapters of Part I: first, an essay-review on nuclear policy which was published in *The New York Review of Books* in August of 1985; second, one entitled 'The Politics of Outer Space', which appeared in June 1985 in *The New Republic*; third, a piece entitled 'Presidents and their Scientific Advisers', which originally appeared as a review in *Minerva*; fourth, an essay to the title 'Scientists, Bureaucrats and Ministers in the UK', which embodies the substance of a 'Friday Evening Discourse' delivered at the Royal Institution in London, and later published in the *Proceedings of the Royal Institution*; and last, the chapter entitled Scientific Advice, which was originally published by the American Philosophical Society in 1980 as 'Science Advisers and Scientific Advisers'.

I would like to express my thanks to the Master and Fellows of Clare College, Cambridge, for the honour of delivering the first E. A. Lane Lecture, and to Mr and Mrs R. Burke Morden and the authorities of the Portland State University for the privilege of delivering the Eighth Keith Morden Lectures. I should also like to express my thanks to the editors of the *New York Review of Books*, *The New Republic*, and *Minerva*; the Royal Institution and the American Philosophical Society for permission to reproduce the various pieces originally published by them; and, as always, to Gillian

Booth and Deirdre Sharp for their unstinting help in preparing the book for the press. I am grateful, too, to Dr Stella Norman for her help in identifying repetitions and suggesting rearrangements in the text, and to Mr William Kimber for the success of his efforts to speed its publication.

LORD ZUCKERMAN
June, 1986

PART
ONE

1

Science, Politics and Social Change

It has become customary to use the term 'technology' to signify the deliberate and systematic exploitation of scientific knowledge, particularly new scientific knowledge, to make things that people need or want. Colour television, satellite communications, antibiotics and computers, are among the fruits of this kind of technology. We have no hesitation in accepting the transforming influence which they exercise on our social lives.

Technology is not, however, some fairy godmother, something outside society. It has always been a mainspring of man's social, political and economic life. Nor is it the case that the course it has taken has always been rationally conceived, to the exclusion of others which in the long run might have proved to be either more or less favourable. Our forebears of the eighteenth century accepted the benefits of the proto-scientific technology of the industrial revolution, in the same unpremeditated way as a prescientific technology had already shaped the basic forms of all our social institutions. The invention of stone implements, and of the spear and bow, the discovery of the wheel—which in turn led not only to the primitive lathe but also to the potter's wheel—the emergence of smelting and metal-working, the invention of the weaving of fibres, the domestication of animals and the cultivation of plants—all these and other major technological developments were steps by which human society has slowly and painfully evolved. Our forebears would never have ended their nomadic life as hunters and food-gatherers had they not discovered the benefits of fixed agriculture and fixed habitations—benefits which some primitive people decided to forgo. Permanent village life would have been precarious if pots had not been invented to store food, water and oil. Co-existence in settlements demanded social rules to which the members of the group adhered in peace. The social life of the village led to the specialisation of labour, to trade, and, through larger settlements, to urbanisation. This social and economic revolution took thousands of years. But at all times the culture of early society reflected its technology, in the same way as the fruits of technology continuously enriched society, both directly and indirectly, providing a basis for man's earliest scientific knowledge, for his art, and for his intellectual development.

In a very genuine sense, society and technology are therefore reflections of each other. The accidental sequence and acceptance of discoveries and invention determined not only the emergence but also the shape of society.

SCIENCE AND TECHNOLOGY

But technology is not science in the classical sense of
that term. To illustrate my conception of the way the
two differ, I have often referred, as I briefly do again,
to the fascinating story of James Watt and the steam-
engine, the main device which powered the industrial
revolution of the eighteenth century.

At the age of twenty-one, Watt, who was born in
Greenock in 1736, became mathematical instrument-
maker to the University in Glasgow. John Robison, a
lecturer in chemistry, and a few years younger than
Watt, drew Watt's attention to the possibility that among
'other purposes', a steam-engine could be used to provide power to move the wheels of carriages. Nothing
of note resulted from this initial stimulus. The spark
was provided by the fact that the University Department
of Natural Philosophy possessed a model of the Newcomen steam engine, an early variety of machine that
used steam to provide power. The model had been sent
to London for repair, but had been returned still not
working properly. In 1763, when he was twenty-seven,
the machine was given to Watt to put in order. Try as
he could, the boiler seemed incapable of providing
enough steam to make the engine run. Yet the full-
scale Newcomen 'fire-engine' (steam-engine) was a de-
pendable machine and, while inefficient in its use of
fuel, was much better than the even-earlier Savery 'steam-
pump' which it was in process of superseding. It was
also a vitally necessary machine. Without it the miner,
because of flooding, could not go on digging deeper for
his coal, or bring to the surface the non-ferrous metal

ores of Cornwall, ores which had been exploited and traded from as far back as Phoenician times.

If Watt had succeeded in making the University's model engine work, he might well have regarded the job as merely one of the chores of an instrument-maker, and that would have been the end of the story. But failure was an intellectual challenge. He set out to discover why it was that so much of the heat and steam produced by the fuel which the engine consumed was wasted. He worked out where and how, and how much heat was being lost, and then embarked upon a systematic study of the relations between the pressure and temperature of steam. At that point Watt ceased to be just an instrument-maker and became a scientist.

His friend Professor Joseph Black then introduced him to the principle of latent heat, which Black had discovered a few years earlier. Watt concluded that the inefficiency of the Newcomen engine was due to a change of state from steam to water inside the working cylinder, and that 'the cylinder should be maintained always as hot as the steam which entered it'. It was on what he called 'a fine Sabbath afternoon' in, it is believed, 1765 (the year does not appear to be precisely recorded), that the solution dawned on him. As he put it, 'the idea came into my mind that as steam was an elastic body it would rush into a vacuum, and if a communication was made between the cylinder and an exhausted vessel, it would rush into it and might be there condensed without cooling the cylinder . . . I had not walked further than the Golf house when the whole thing was arranged in my mind.'[1]

The 'whole thing' was a separate condenser into which steam was made to escape from the working cylinder. This was the turning point. But it took ten more years of hard work before he had devised an adequate industrial engine, and before, this time as a technologist, he had made all the supplementary inventions which had to go with it—the governor to control the speed of the engine, and the indicator, which he invented with the help of John Southern. The machine that emerged was the prototype of a host of steam-engines which were developed for a variety of different purposes.

The story of James Watt shows clearly that technology can leap well ahead of the basic science from which, *post hoc*, it seems to derive. At the start Watt knew nothing about latent heat, but he knew in his bones what was wrong with the Newcomen engine and, as a scientist, he then saw the way to cure its defects. At the moment of his inspiration, when the solution to his problem flashed through his mind, his attention could have been focused only on the vision of a separate condenser, in the same way as in the years that followed, while well aware of the potential industrial value of his invention, his thoughts could seldom have strayed from the further technical problems that had to be solved before he had produced an efficient steam-engine.

His financial backers, amongst whom Matthew Boulton, a highly successful scientific industrialist of Birmingham, was the most prominent, were interested in the technicalities, but their minds were probably focused far more on the possible industrial applications of the engine and, in the first instance, on devising a source of power for the pumps for which the mines in Cornwall were crying out. Doubtlessly, too, as happens today, Watt's backers were worrying about the time the project was taking and about the money it was costing. But beyond speculating about the possible applications of steam-power for factory machinery and locomotives, I doubt very much if a single one of the small number of people who were directly concerned ever gave a thought to the wider social and political consequences of steam-power. They were as ignorant of the enormous social transformations it would bring about as were the people whose lives were going to be so profoundly affected. As is almost always the case, that part was left to history. And if the story of the steam-engine is typical, and I think it is, it shows that the social repercussions of those major technological innovations that happen to catch on are usually unpredictable and, in consequence, usually uncontrollable.

CHANCE AND SCIENTIFIC DISCOVERY

The story of James Watt also shows that while one can discuss the methods of science in precise terms, there is nothing very orderly, and therefore predictable, about the process of scientific discovery itself. The most far-reaching advances in the history of science are rare. They seem just to have happened, unpredictably, shaking the framework of current belief, before, like Isaac Newton's laws of motion and gravitation, or Charles

Darwin's theory of natural selection, or Albert Einstein's general theory of relativity, they permeate and transform prevailing belief, and reveal new horizons for intellectual enquiry.

New scientific understanding may emerge as a by-product of a piece of practical engineering, as in Watt's case, where most of the new science was revealed by men who had not been directly involved in the technological development of the engine. It was Clerk Maxwell, years after, who worked out the theory of Watt's governor, and in so doing provided the start of the modern science of control-engineering. Some historians go so far as to say that Watt's methods of measuring engine power also started a line of experimentation and thought which eventually produced the laws of thermodynamics, and so led, some even say, to the quantum theory.

There are also examples in the history of science of fundamentally new areas of scientific understanding being opened up by a scientist who had applied his mind to the task of solving a practical problem. One of the most celebrated examples is provided by Louis Pasteur's enquiries into the problem of fermentation. Pasteur was already an experienced research chemist when he directed his attention to the fact that deleterious fermentation sometimes occurs in wine and beer. The results of the experimental work which he undertook to find out why this happened were as far-reaching to our basic understanding of the behaviour of micro-organisms as were those revealed by the more straightforward bacteriological researches of his two contemporaries, Robert Koch and F.J. Cohn. It is to these three men that we owe the foundation for our understanding of a variety of disease processes—an understanding that also helped transform our social lives.

Another example of basic scientific knowledge being used to provide an answer to a practical problem, and one which relates to today's era of 'high-tech', was the deliberate search by the Bell Laboratories for an alternative to the thermionic valve used in radio and radar. The objective was to invent a miniaturised amplifier which could resist shocks and vibration, which the valve could not tolerate. As the story goes, William Shockley decided to base his search on what was known about the wave-like movement of electrons in semiconducting crystals. The outcome is that today we have the transistor. This led to the electronic computer and to a host of other developments which have changed our lives and which, at the same time, have opened up new fields of basic scientific enquiry.

Shockley's invention of the transistor earned him a Nobel Prize. It was a just reward for a lengthy and methodical intellectual enquiry whose outcome very quickly transformed the whole field of communications. But inventions almost as far-reaching in their effects have been made by scientists in almost casual fashion. One of the best examples of which I know is John Randall's cavity-magnetron, a small radio-valve which early in the Second World War made microwave radar possible—and so helped prevent the defeat of Britain by Hitler's Germany. That invention certainly did not come about as a result of the kind of methodical enquiry pursued by Shockley.

When Winston Churchill said that, 'Never in the field of human conflict was so much owed by so many to so few,' he was referring to the Battle of Britain. It was won in 1940 by the Royal Air Force largely because the British had integrated radar into an operational early-warning and command system before the Luftwaffe launched their assault on England. But in those days the range at which radar could pick up enemy aircraft was limited, and the wavelength—about 50m—nowhere near what was operationally desirable. The best of Britain's physicists were hard at work trying to find an effective way of getting rid of these major and, at the time, highly dangerous and critical shortcomings.

John Randall was a young physicist who had been drafted into war work, and who had been attached to a small team at the University of Birmingham which, in parallel with others in different parts of the country, was then trying to make microwave radar possible. Within a matter of weeks he suddenly saw that the way to solve the problem was to combine two principles which were then being investigated separately—and vainly—by different teams of physicists. The result was a relatively small valve which could generate microwaves with sufficient power to give range. This discovery was immensely important to both the British and American Air Forces. It also had several other uses, particularly in anti-submarine warfare. But to Randall the time he had spent on the task was, as he put it, an 'interlude' in his scientific life, into which he had been 'reluctantly dragged', and which he ended with relief. In 1943, as soon as he could be released, he moved for the rest of the war to a teaching job in Cambridge. He died in

1984—one of England's most distinguished biophysicists.

One of Pasteur's much-quoted phrases is that 'in the field of observation chance only favours those who are prepared'. In the search that led him to the transistor, Shockley was prepared by his familiarity with quantum mechanics. But being prepared does not mean just being steeped in the body of all relevant and available knowledge. Sometimes, as several chapters in the history of science show, traditional scientific doctrine and scientific fashion may become a hindrance to the acceptance of something which is both new and true. Or, to put it another way, scientists can be ahead of their time.

One famous instance is the history of the highly important kinetic theory of gases. This was clearly formulated in 1845 by a man named Waterston,[2] but because the paper which he submitted to the Royal Society did not fit the conventional wisdom of the day, it was suppressed for nearly half a century. Waterston, in turn, had based his enquiries on the equally spurned work of a self-educated mathematician named Herapath, who in 1820 also had a paper rejected by the Royal Society. This instructive story was revealed to the world by Lord Rayleigh, a renowned physicist of the day, and at the time the Secretary of the Royal Society. The preface which he provided for Waterston's paper when it finally appeared in print in 1893, nearly fifty years after it had been submitted for publication, begins with the memorable words: 'The publication of this paper after nearly half a century demands a word of explanation.' Rayleigh then went on to say that his own attention had been drawn to Waterston's work when reading a short account which the latter had published in 1851 in another journal, and which 'distinctly stated the law, which was afterwards to become so famous, of the equality of the kinetic energies of different molecules at the same temperature. . . . The omission to publish it at the time was a misfortune, which probably retarded the development of the subject by ten or fifteen years.'[3]

Here it is worth noting that the mathematical principles and logic on which the modern computer is based had been clearly formulated well over a century ago by Charles Babbage, a pillar of the British establishment of the early nineteenth century, and the founder of the Royal Astronomical and Statistical Societies. Babbage must have been one of the first recipients of a government R&D grant in any country. But because of the limitations of the wheel-and-rod machinery which was available to him, he was unable to develop the 'calculating machine', the potential power of which he could clearly visualise. His ideas were far and away ahead of the technological possibilities of the day. Not until H.H. Aiken of Harvard employed electromagnetic relays were Babbage's principles first put into effect— well over a hundred years after they were formulated.

As one reflects on the names and discoveries to which I have referred, or for that matter on the names of other scientists and technologists who have helped change the face of the earth, one gets the feeling that everything could easily have turned out totally differently from the way it did. Had James Watt not hit upon the idea of a separate condenser, the history of the industrial revolution of the latter half of the eighteenth century would have been different from what it was. The significance of the kinetic theory of gases might have been appreciated in the earlier and not the later part of the nineteenth century. Animal and plant breeders might have understood the value of Mendel's simple laws of genetics twenty years before they did. Shockley might not have thought of electron transfer in semiconductor crystals. Indeed, there might have been no Einstein—any more than one can predict when there will be another like him, one whose penetrating mind can comprehend relationships that have never been imagined before, relationships that embrace scores of previously understood relationships.

One cannot predict when those major leaps forward in science, those from which all the rest follow, will occur, any more than one can predict strokes of technological genius.

If that is one of the lessons which I would draw from the history of those scientific discoveries whose exploitation has helped transform our world, what then about the power of the state to direct science in politically chosen directions or, to use what seems now to be a fashionable term, 'to command technology'?

TECHNOLOGY AS AN INSTRUMENT OF THE STATE

It is not so many years since the emphasis I have been placing on the part that chance plays in scientific and

technological discovery would have drawn a strong protest from a school of thought which held that the direction of scientific discovery, and the very nature of
those discoveries, can be related to the social and economic milieu within which they emerge—in time as
well as place. Francis Bacon, that extraordinary mixture
of statesman, courtier and philosopher of the late sixteenth and early seventeenth centuries, who with Des-
cartes founded modern rational philosophy, spelt out
in his *New Atlantis* an imaginary picture of an ideal
state which was ruled by scientific sages, who themselves decided what 'secrets' they would reveal to the
administrative machine of the State. Bacon's view of
science was overwhelmingly utilitarian; to him knowledge and power were the same. His picture[4] of a rational
relation of science to society may well have been mere
wishful-thinking, but years later the same vision was
revealed to the Western world as a communist blueprint
for science. The story is interesting.

During the first ten years or so following the 1917
Revolution, those Russian scientists who had not left
the country continued to work as they had before. By
the end of the twenties, however, all Russian scientists
had, in effect, been made servants of the State. Even
the Academy of Sciences was politicised. These changes
were explained to the Western world in 1931 at the
Second International Congress of the History of Science. The meeting took place in London, and among
those who attended were a number of prominent Russian scientists and politicians. One of them, Boris Hessen, caused a considerable stir by arguing that the stimulus

for Isaac Newton's enquiries into matters such as gravitation and the laws of motion was a number of practical
problems that related to the rise of capitalism. Hessen
was not claiming that Newton's analytical methods were
inspired by economic factors. The point he was making
was that what he called the 'earthy core' of Newton's
Principia comprised technical problems related to mining, ballistics, hydrostatics, magnetism, optics and mechanics. And the moral which he drew from his analysis
was that science cannot advance in a society which
restricts technological advance. 'Science develops out
of production, and those social forms which become
fetters upon productive forces likewise become fetters
upon science.'[5]

Hessen's analysis, which most historians today regard as far-fetched, impressed several prominent British
scientists who were at the meeting, and who were ready
to promote the view that science needs to be organised
in a way which furthers its social function. Not surprisingly, a group of equally distinguished British scientists reacted by forming a Society for Freedom in
Science. I had friends in both camps, and I believed
then, as I still do, that both were tilting at windmills.

It happened, however, that this particular debate
about free or directed science was taking place in the
thirties, in a period when fascism was on the rise in
Europe, and when scientists in Germany were being
persecuted as well as coerced. And it was also the period
of World War II, so that in Britain, too, scientists who
were not directly involved with the armed services were
necessarily directed to essential national employment.

But the moment the fighting stopped, so too did the direction of British scientists, with the President of the Royal Society enjoining scientists in universities not to undertake any more work which was secret. However, the peace that came was not the peace of earlier years. The State still had need of scientists—in industry, in universities, and in government laboratories—and scientific education was accordingly encouraged by successive British governments. In view of the enormous resources which consequently had to be diverted to the promotion of science and technology, it was also realised that there had to be some central coordination. An Advisory Council on Scientific Policy was set up and, at least on paper, national science policies became the order of the day. But British scientists were still free. They could still choose their field of employment or, if they so wished, they could abandon science altogether.

What was happening in Britain in the years after World War II mirrored events in other countries, including the United States. The only US Federal institution which existed before World War II to which the Government could turn for expert help was the National Research Council. This Council had been set up during the first world war as the executive arm of the National Academy of Sciences, the body which had been founded by President Lincoln at the time of the Civil War. In 1940, President Roosevelt established a National Defense Research Committee to complement the National Research Council, and a year later an Office of Scientific Research and Development—OSRD for short—'to coordinate the scientific activity of the United States on a national scale in an all-out war effort'. Dr Vannevar Bush, of MIT and the Carnegie Institution in Washington, was made its Chairman.

The President was so impressed by the success of this body that, before the war ended, he asked Dr Bush to provide a blueprint for an institution which would carry on with the task of coordinating America's scientific effort in peacetime. Dr Bush's recommendations, which in due course were partly realised in the shape of the present National Science Foundation, were strikingly utilitarian in flavour. They called for a national policy, and for high-level planning, for science, in terms far bolder and more materialistic than had ever been used by any member of the scientific establishment in Britain. Bush wanted science to be brought to what he called the centre of the stage, and for it to be provided with a policy which would ensure its rapid growth in the interests of the State.

This seemed strikingly similar to what one assumed to be the policy of the USSR. Indeed, when the arms-race was accelerating in the 1950s, Dr Edwin Land, one of President Eisenhower's scientific advisers, and a billiant scientist and innovator, warned the President that because so much was being done by large groups of scientists and by the State itself, 'more and more we [the United States] tend to resemble the Soviets, however much we disclaim this.'[6] Professor McDougall, by whom these words are quoted, and who has devoted much critical thought to the issue of what he calls 'state-driven technological change', also quotes

Horace Gray, an economist, as saying that the United States now socializes the financing of research, but permits what he called 'private monopolization of its output . . . The end product is an institutional monstrosity—a bastard form of socialism crossbred with a bastard form of capitalism.'

These are colourful words, but there can be no doubt that in the years since the start of the second world war all industrialised countries, not just the UK and the USA, have tried to harness science in the interests of the State. President Eisenhower once declared that science is 'the servant and handmaiden of the freedom which is the central ideal of Western democracy'. Obviously it is also the servant and handmaiden of authoritarian regimes—even if, as we believe, it is not as efficient a servant as it is in Western societies. In their various ways, all countries now try to make science and technology an instrument of the State—some more successfully than others. Robert Lewis has described[7] how the Soviet administrative system for science and technology is changed repeatedly in the effort to make it more effective. The same is happening in other countries.

But perhaps President Eisenhower's description of science as a handmaiden was not really very appropriate. In the days when servants and handmaidens were not in as short supply as they now are, one could order them to do something and expect the order to be carried out. Can one say the same of science? Can Presidents command science? As Hotspur put it in *Henry IV*, any man can call spirits from the vasty deep, 'but will they

come when you do call for them?' Will they come
when the State commands? Can the State really rely
on getting the results it wants from science and technology? Can science be directed from the centre? Above
all, can one hope to control the unpredictable social
consequences of major scientific and technological advances?

COMMANDING TECHNOLOGY

Soon after President Nixon moved to the White House,
he proclaimed to the world that he hoped to eradicate
cancer during the years he was President. Relatively
enormous resources were made available for research,
but cancer is still with us. Earlier on President Kennedy
undertook to put a man on the moon. The Apollo
programme succeeded. Why the one and not the other?
And now we have President Reagan's SDI.

The reason that President Kennedy's initiative succeeded and President Nixon's failed is, I think, fairly
straightforward. President Kennedy's daring undertaking depended both on the outstanding courage of the
astronauts concerned and on knowledge that was already there. The time was ripe for it. No new scientific
principles were involved. The task which he set NASA
was that of putting available knowledge to work through
precise and brilliant engineering. And the whole thing
worked—first time. President Nixon, on the other hand,
was calling on knowledge that simply was not there—
and is not with us yet. The time was unripe, as it was
when Babbage enunciated the logical principles of the

modern computer. Whether the time is ripe for SDI is discussed in Chapter Four.

Significant breakthroughs in pure or fundamental science cannot be commanded. Strokes of genius cannot be commissioned either in science or in any other form of creative activity. No one could have commanded Beethoven to compose his Ninth Symphony, any more than a clerk called Einstein working in the Patent Office in Berlin could have been told to get busy and devise a general theory of relativity. The best that a central authority can do when dealing with the unknown, with what has not yet been created, is provide resources which those who are recognised as having the necessary competence would be free to use in pursuing their own ideas. Of course such a measure could never guarantee success, any more than it would be easy for a democratic state to devise a system of support which helped only the élite among all who would like to be regarded as such.

The prospects for successful direction are much more favourable when we are dealing with technology. All countries try to promote technical improvements in weaponry, in public services such as water supplies and roads, in health, and sometimes in agriculture. Here one expects minor developments all the time. Sometimes, of course, the State can make far-reaching mistakes, such as happened in the USSR during the thirties, when Stalin suppressed scientific genetics, and set Soviet agriculture back for decades by encouraging the false teachings on animal and plant breeding which were fostered by Michurin and Lysenko. This is not the only instance of governmental direction of technology which has had untoward, even disastrous, results.

Of course it is not just government which issues commands to the scientific and technological community. Industry does so all the time, for success in the market place is dependent on innovation, and innovation in turn depends on R&D. The Ten Commandments were formulated to help regulate social behaviour in the small and isolated agrarian society of ancient Israel. One Commandment enjoins us not to covet 'anything that is thy neighbour's'. Today we are encouraged to covet. Advertising, which has become part of our lives, tells us what to covet. The demand of the market has become a powerful driving force behind technological innovation. The process can be disguised by many catch-phrases but, whatever else, it cannot be stopped.

As is also all too clear, not all innovations turn out to be unmixed blessings, either in the short- or in the long-term. New drugs may be licensed for use, and a few, like thalidomide, turn out to be highly dangerous. New agricultural practices may be introduced in order to increase productivity, but some turn out to have highly undesirable ecological and environmental consequences. In order to deal with these, the State has to establish monitoring agencies such as the Environmental Protection Agency and the Food and Drugs Administration in the United States. The direct or internal costs of industrial developments, including what it takes to get them to the market, thus tell only part of the story of the costs of innovation. The coincidental or external costs are something extra. When the automobile emerged at the start of our century, it was a boon and a blessing to the few who could afford to buy one. In the years since then, a car has become a necessity of life for most of us. But look what it has cost the State in roads, in congestion, in pollution, and in lives. None of the unfortunate by-products of the internal combustion engine was envisaged when the automobile-age began.

RESPONSIBILITY

Many have asked where responsibility rests for the coincidental but deleterious by-products which often result from technological innovation. My own view is that it cannot be laid upon the shoulders of scientists who open up those new horizons of understanding which encourage the generation of novel technological ideas. It can be argued, however, and it is argued, that responsibility should rest on the shoulders of those by whom the exploitation was encouraged—whether it be private industry or government. That, I believe, is what the Common Law recognises. But I doubt whether the implementation of the law could ever be made consistent in a democratic society.

In 1959 I delivered the Commencement Address at the California Institute of Technology, to the theme of 'Liberty in an age of science'.[8] One of the points I made was that 'the untrammelled emergence of new scientific ideas is not compatible with any restraint on

the liberty of the scientist to roam where his fancy leads'.
I was using the term 'liberty' to imply an individual's
right to live and act freely within the compass of the
institutions which the society of which he is a member
will have set up in the exercise of its sovereign power.
Over the years I have, however, learnt that the traditional and abstract concept of sovereign power is mostly
fiction. In today's world the ways by which a theoret-
ically uninhibited sovereign power expresses itself are
more and more determined by the impact of science
and technology. The liberty we enjoy in an age of
science has been liberty of a kind, but it is liberty within
the framework created by the technology that we exploit.

I concluded my address with a paragraph which
began with the statement that, 'Science, technology and
humanism seem to have assumed that order of importance in the determination of our affairs', and which
ended by saying, 'What we most need to learn is that
in the major scientific matters which now affect human
destiny, one cannot safely take decisions for today unless we realize that those same decisions determine the
future. This realization may not lead to the right decisions; but it might help obviate some of the worse.'
Where does this thought lead when we consider the
issue of responsibility?

Richard Crossman, who died in 1974, was a prominent British politician and one-time academic. He is
also celebrated for having left behind a diary of his life
as a Cabinet Minister which is probably more detailed
than that of any other British politician, including even

Churchill and Macmillan. When referring to the general problem of how decisions are taken about technological matters, he asked, 'How can a Cabinet come to a sensible decision when none of us has the vaguest idea what these things really are?'[9] This sobering thought had not occurred to him when, as a teacher at Oxford during the thirties, he wrote a book to the title *Government and the Governed*.[10] It required the experience of hard political responsibility for him to realise the enormous importance of the issue.

For the first time this century, the United Kingdom has a Prime Minister who was trained as a scientist, and who for a short time worked as a research chemist in industry. But not a single one of her predecessors was a scientist, and she herself has spent the better part of her working life as a politician. I do not believe that the United States has ever had a President who was educated as a scientist. It is, however, the President's responsibility to choose and then appoint—given the sanction of the Senate—the members of his cabinet. The question is, How does he choose his scientists? What constitutes scientific literacy in the upper reaches of Government?

It is now more than twenty-five years since I delivered my Caltech Address. It was very obvious then that the world was in a phase of rapid change. We were entering a tumultuous post-colonial era, and a new problem, that of the Third World, was emerging. Differential and, in places, explosive population growth was changing the demographic map. There was a threat of a host of environmental problems which had not been faced before. But above all, it was the 'cold war' between East and West that was then uppermost in our minds, with all the signs pointing to an acceleration of the nuclear arms-race.

And the arms-race has indeed accelerated over these past twenty-five years. It has absorbed enormous resources. Yet, paradoxically, national security seems to have lessened everywhere. Can we have been taking the right decisions? Can we be confident now that we shall obviate the worst? Are we now for the last time at the crossroads where we can choose to take the road that is marked 'a safe peace'? Or are we to be impelled along the one that leads to even more perilous nuclear minefields than those through which we have had to weave our way these past three decades? And who should we blame for the decisions that led us into the minefields, and on whose shoulders does responsibility rest for the wiser decisions that need to be taken now if we are to progress to a less perilous future—those of our political leaders, of our military leaders, or of scientists who advise them?

Clearly, final responsibility, and therefore blame, must rest on the political authority. But if any useful lessons are to be drawn from the past, those who wield the authority will always have to beware of technical military advisers whose vision is constrained within the ruts of past decision, of advisers who are obsessed by narrow vested interests and by new contrivances which are irrelevant to the real situation that we now face. This is asking a lot, both of those who accept advice and those who tender it. But it is something that must be asked. I return to this point in Chapter Eight.

REFERENCES

1. Crowther, J.G., 1962, *Scientists of the Industrial Revolution*, London: Cresset Press, p. 123.
2. Brush, S.G., 1959, The development of the kinetic theory of gases II. Waterston, *Ann. Sci.*, **13**, 273.
3. Waterston, J.J., 1893, *Phil. Trans. R. Soc.*, **183A**, 5.
4. It is supposed to have influenced the attitude of the members of the Invisible College which, tradition has it, was the precursor of the Royal Society in 1660.
5. *Science at the Crossroads* (papers from the International Congress of the History of Science and Technology, 1931), 1971, London: Frank Cass.
6. McDougall, Walter A., 1985, *The Heavens and the Earth*, New York: Basic Books.
7. Lewis, R., 1984, *Minerva*, **22**, 129–159.
8. Zuckerman, S., 1959, *Nature, Lond.*, **184**, 135.
9. Crossman, Richard, 1976, *Diaries of a Cabinet Minister*, **2**, London: Hamish Hamilton, p. 126.
10. London: Christophers, 1939 and 1947.

2

The Arms Race and National Security

The association of the profession of arms with the world of science is usually seen as a development of the second world war. In fact there has always been an association. In the far distant past were the craftsmen of the stone and iron ages who fashioned spears and arrows out of materials which they judged the best for their purposes. In the fourteenth and fifteenth centuries, makers of armaments included sophisticated metallurgists and artificers, many of whose names, such as that of Leonardo da Vinci, have become part of history.[1] Even before Leonardo, the profession of armourer was well established both in Europe and Asia. In England the office of Master of the King's Ordnance, later styled Master-General, was established as early as 1414. It was the start of the British Ordnance Board, an institution which still exists. The office of Master-General also still continues, although he is no longer President of the Board; nor does he enjoy—as he did until the year 1828—a seat in the Cabinet. In the light of the nuclear dangers which now hang over the world, it is perhaps a pity that cabinets and politburos do not still include in their number someone who knows at first hand about the enormous destructive power of modern armaments.

SCIENTISTS AND SOLDIERS

Despite their traditional dependence on the technological arts, professional military men have usually been cautious about new ideas which challenge custom and tradition. That is why it is so commonly said that generals are always preparing to fight the next war as though it were the last. Doubtlessly, too, there were admirals in navies other than the British who protested against the replacement of sail by steam, or the semaphore by radio. In World War II a story used to be told about an up-to-date and technically-minded general who, in the course of inspecting a mechanised gun-battery, spotted a solitary soldier standing to attention some yards from, and with his back to, the nearest gun. 'And what is that man doing?' he asked. 'He's steadying the horses,' was the reply.

If the tale is apocryphal, it nonetheless carries a message. The essence of any military organisation must be law and order, rigid discipline and loyalty. Without them, men could never be ordered to face death in battle—as Tennyson put it, 'Their's not to reason why, their's but to do and die.' But a scientist has to reason, has to question, has to doubt. If he does not question the prevailing corpus of scientific knowledge, he is no true scientist. There will always be this dichotomy between the two professions.

This fact was not very apparent before the emergence of radar in the thirties. Until then, military men were brought up in the same environment as the one in which their armaments were fashioned. They had their own ordnance factories, their own engineers and sappers, their own ship-yards, even their own service-trained medical men. The intrusion of radar changed all this. It is a strange fact that the Germans had already developed technically better radar sets than ours. What they had not done was devise a direction-finding and tracking system, similar to the one which British scientists had helped put together for the RAF. It was this that transformed radar from a simple early-warning system into an effective instrument of command.

During the Second World War, civilian scientists were responsible for countless technical developments, including, to mention only three, sonar (a first world war scientific development), navigational devices, and electronic countermeasures. And of course there was 'the bomb'. Another considerable scientific contribution, but not in the form of hardware, was the development of operational research. In the days of World War II, it entailed the observation and study of actual events, as opposed to the analysis of abstract situations and *in vacuo* models of the kind which now characterise so much of the subject. Wartime operational research transformed the technical and the tactical, and even on occasion, the strategic scene.

Another point that should be noted here is that until the end of World War II, there was little difficulty in accommodating new technical ideas and weaponry within accepted tactical and strategic military doctrine.

The new developments did not conflict, for example, with traditional views about the value of surprise and of preemptive attack, or about the need to be able to outflank and outmanoeuvre an enemy, to outgun and silence his guns, to slow down his reinforcements, to cut his lines of communications, and to protect one's own. When they first appeared, even nuclear weapons and ballistic missiles seemed compatible with normal doctrine. During the four to five years when atom bombs were only in US hands, they were usually regarded as merely representing additional, even if remarkably excessive, fire-power. Ballistic missiles, with good guidance systems and range, were also accepted into conventional armouries without any strain on current military doctrine.

NUCLEAR WEAPONS IN MILITARY OPERATIONS

This state of innocence lasted no longer than the few years that it took the USSR to reveal that it too had the bomb, that it too had ballistic missiles. But it has taken many more for either side even to begin to come to terms with the reality that no *military* doctrine can be sufficiently transformed to accommodate nuclear weapons—in particular, no acceptable doctrine as it applies to a potential land-war between the NATO and the Warsaw Pact powers. The world has become progressively more dangerous during the time the two sides have shut their eyes to this basic fact—despite the efforts of a small number of perceptive military men, who immediately recognised that once the USSR had the capability to retaliate in kind to a nuclear attack, the bomb ceased to be a military weapon. It could be likened to a pistol which fires backwards as well as forwards when the trigger is squeezed. Unfortunately, there were too few realists around to stem the enthusiasm of the civilian nuclear warriors who were only too ready to provide eager military buyers with new destructive wares.

I am ignorant of the way matters are organised in the USSR, but from what I know of the situation in the United States and the United Kingdom, I would judge that rarely, if ever, are new nuclear designs put forward in response to clearly thought-out *military* operational requirements. They are usually the brain-children of the weaponeers themselves. So it was that nuclear land-mines were designed and turned out regardless of the reactions of the European political authorities on whose land they were to be planted. Low-yield nuclear artillery-shells and other weapons for short-range use —by which is meant a range of, say, up to thirty miles—were deployed in Europe without any proper consideration of what their effects would be on both sides were they ever used.

It has only recently come to light that the United States has apparently not tested more than a single nuclear artillery-shell in the atmosphere (if the Russians ever tested one, they have never made the fact public). The weapon had a yield of 17 kt (approximately the same yield as that of the bomb which effaced Hiroshima), and was detonated six miles from the emplacement from which it was fired. Bernard J. O'Keefe, one of the survivors of the group of twenty-five men involved in the test, has described what happened. The fireball mounted thousands of feet into the air and the shock-wave was felt ninety miles away.

> The first flash, he writes,[1] would sear the eye-balls of anyone looking in that direction, friend or foe, for miles around. Its intensity cannot be described; it must be experienced to be appreciated. The electromagnetic pulse would knock out all communication systems, the life blood of a battle plan. In addition to its effects on troops in the vicinity, everyone for fifty miles in any direction who lived through it would realize that it was a nuclear explo-sion. It would seem like the end of the world, and it probably would be, for any man who had a similar weapon under his control, who had a button to push or a lanyard to pull, would do so instinctively.[2]

This, one should note, is what a single nuclear deto-nation would do. A nuclear battle would mean not one but scores, hundreds, of shells and bombs, many, be-cause of their greater yields, even more devastating than the 17 kt artillery-shell which was tested. Quite apart from Mr O'Keefe's observations, analyses of several 'war-games' and field-manoeuvres since the late fifties on-wards have indicated that a nuclear battle on European soil would inevitably result in military stalemate and enormous losses, as well as millions of civilian deaths. Mainland Europe, with all its cities, towns and villages, is densely populated. Fourteen kt on Hiroshima killed 80,000 people. A megaton on any large city would immediately kill more than half a million people. It defies all imagination to conceive of a battle zone in which scores and scores of nuclear shells and bombs would be exploding, in which towns presumed to be 'interdiction' targets disappear in a flash, in which nothing can move, in which only death rules. That is what nuclear 'war' would mean.

It is hardly surprising that no one has ever devised a scenario of a tactical nuclear battle that makes sense. There are so-called NATO guidelines which define the circumstances in which the Supreme Commander might be authorised to initiate a nuclear attack. There are none which tell how a nuclear battle could proceed or, once started, how stopped.

Nonetheless, and basically because they constitute very powerful explosive devices, nuclear weapons were stocked in Western Europe for presumed battlefield use from about the mid-fifties—with barely a single responsible field commander convinced that, once they were fired, he would be able to control the consequences of their use, or that he could guarantee that what started as destruction on a field of battle would not result in limitless destruction of the homelands of all the powers engaged.

NATO commanders of the fifties used to declare that if attacked they would strike at their Soviet opponents with all the nuclear armaments at their disposal. As Field-Marshal Montgomery, the Deputy Supreme Commander to General Eisenhower, put it, were NATO forces to be attacked, it wasn't a case of whether the new weapons would be used; they would be used, adding for emphasis, 'I'll strike first and seek permission afterwards.'

But this has long since ceased to be the cry. For example, all but four of the nine distinguished British officers who during the period since 1957 have filled the high office of Chief of the British Defence Staff (the tenth is now in post), have declared publicly that the idea of fighting and winning a nuclear ·war in Europe makes no sense. Other NATO commanders, both European and American, as well as Soviet military chiefs, have said the same thing. Those who in the early days tried to tell the NATO Command that reliance on nuclear weapons meant that the Supreme Commander, like the Emperor, had no clothes, received no more than an encouraging nod of the head. Liddell Hart, remembered by many as the foremost student and analyst of military history of this century, and a practical strategist and tactician of considerable experience, was convinced from the start that so-called tactical nuclear weapons were of little value in relation to the risks they entailed.[3]

NUCLEAR DOCTRINE

What is supposed to be military doctrine about nuclear weapons has now become a tissue of wishful thoughts and slogans. The fact is that no field commander in the European theatre could give his political masters an assurance that a war in which nuclear weapons were used could remain 'limited'. The only scenario which could, in theory, justify such an assurance would be the inconceivable one in which the two sides were performing like partners in a practised minuet, exchanging units of destructive force in a measured way—that is to say, eliminating each other's airfields and cities, and killing millions of citizens—both then stopping by mutual agreement before they were completely wiped out.

Nuclear weapons were invented, not because the military were crying out for them, but because a group of knowledgeable physicists knew that weight for weight they would be thousands of times more destructive than conventional bombs. There were few, if indeed any, political or military leaders who at the start knew enough about nuclear physics to understand why this was so. They encouraged the development simply because, during the Second World War, bigger and more destructive bombs were always assumed to be something worth having. The scientists who were involved did not, however, succeed in making it clear that there is a vast difference between bombs whose destructive effects are due to a rearrangement of molecules and atoms, as occurs in a conventional 'chemical' explosion, and the destructive nuclear force resulting from the release of the huge amounts of energy which bind together the constituent sub-atomic particles that make up the atom, and so matter.

Today the only justification given for the deployment of so-called battlefield or theatre nuclear weapons is that they confer reality on the twin policy of nuclear deterrence and 'flexible response'. By the first is meant that they constitute a warning to the USSR that they might be used to counter any Soviet intrusion into Europe. By the second is meant that NATO would counter any such intrusion with whatever level of force proved necessary, starting at the lower end of the scale with foot-soldiers and moving on, if needs be, to the use of nuclear weapons.

Both terms, 'deterrence' and 'flexible response' are little more than verbal rationalisations of a prevailing situation. Neither implies any revolutionary military concept. Deterrence and aggression have always been opposite sides of the same coin—or, as the French put it, *'Cet animal est très méchant. Quand on l'attaque, il se défend.'* Flexible response is indeed no more than one of many ways of stating the hallowed and somewhat theoretical military doctrine of the economy of force, which implies that a military commander would never use more force than is necessary to achieve whatever objective he had been set; and that he would resort to the use of nuclear weapons only if an attack could not be countered by his conventional forces. The term— first called 'full options policy'—was in effect a reassuring euphemism which some cynics said that Mr McNamara, when Defense Secretary, had coined to allay European fears that were the Soviets to attack, the immediate response would not accord with the 1954 doctrine of 'massive nuclear retaliation' against the mainland of the USSR, of a kind which would provoke an equivalent strike against Western Europe. As Foster Dulles, when Secretary of State, put it, the United

States would retaliate against military action hostile to American interest, 'instantly, by means and at places of our own choosing'.[4] To some extent, but not entirely, this doctrine reflected a realisation that the European members of NATO would be either unable or unwilling to muster enough conventional force to contain a Soviet attack. 'Massive nuclear retaliation' was thus also the expression of a belief that weakness in conventional arms could be compensated for by nuclear weapons.

As the decade of the fifties ended, it became more and more obvious, however, that if the USSR were to suffer a massive nuclear attack she would reply in kind, not only against the European members of NATO but also against the American mainland. By 1960, a state of mutual nuclear deterrence had started to prevail. To the public the turning point was the Cuban missile crisis of 1962.

Nonetheless, there was no stopping the nuclear arms-race. A popular belief had been encouraged that numbers of bombs matter, and that the USA had to have enough weapons in its armoury to inflict what was euphemistically called 'unacceptable damage' on the USSR, by which was meant it had to be able to eliminate in a nuclear attack a quarter of the Soviet population and to destroy half its industrial capacity.

This criterion of 'unacceptable damage' was arbitrary. It was no more than a recognition of the theoretical destructive capacity of the nuclear armaments which the Americans already deployed or had in the pipeline. When Robert McNamara became American Defense Secretary in 1961, he agreed with the implicit numerical definition of 'unacceptable damage' as a way of checking irrational and arbitrary demands from the American Chiefs of Staff for ever more nuclear armaments. The complementary phrase, 'mutually assured destruction', was also coined when it was accepted at the political level that either side had the power to destroy its adversary, regardless of who struck first, and whatever the circumstances in which he struck.

The concept of unacceptable damage was essentially an American one, the product of the calculations of armchair civilian strategists who, unlike the Russians, had little or no experience of the reality of massive destruction. The American Air Force chiefs had their allies in Congress, and were unprepared to accept a more modest and realistic definition of 'unacceptable damage'. And President Kennedy, who in the election campaign of 1960 had repeatedly proclaimed that the previous administration had weakened America by allowing the Russians to forge ahead in the development of ballistic missiles, knew that in matters of this sort, presidential authority—even after he had learnt that the 'missile gap' was a myth—had to bow to congressional and public pressure.

The Russians said little or nothing in the early sixties. They listened and became persuaded that the United States was bent on destroying their homeland with 'a bolt from the blue', in a 'first strike' by nuclear weapons. Not surprisingly, they reacted by building up their forces, doubtlessly also encouraged by their own theorists and map-targeteers. The upshot was that, according to American calculations in the early sixties,

by the end of the decade the USSR would have had
enough of its nuclear forces intact after all its 'targetable'
units had been destroyed by an American pre-
emptive strike, to retaliate with an attack calculated to
kill at least half the American population.

LOOSENING THE DEADLOCK

Obviously the USA and the USSR did not embark on
a joint exercise to reach a state of nuclear stalemate.
But in retrospect one can see that it was inevitable that
this would happen, and that stalemate would characterise every situation in which the armed forces of the
East faced those of the West. Up to now, every attempt
to break the nuclear deadlock has failed. A long series
of arms-control negotiations, on which I shall touch in
the following chapter, have not made any significant
dent in the problem. The belief that because technology
got us into the present nuclear mess, technology should
get us out of it, has also proved an empty hope. Indeed,
it has made the problem worse by exacerbating the
arms-race.

The search for a technical solution to the stalemate
has taken two forms: first, a quest for ways by which
the other side's nuclear weapons can be destroyed; and
second, for means to nullify a nuclear attack. Neither
approach has proved successful—or even promises any
success—despite endless effort.

The essence of the concept of nuclear deterrence
is that no rational nuclear power would attack an opponent if doing so carried the risk of being destroyed
by a retaliatory nuclear attack. In theory, but in theory

only, the problem of the possible vulnerability of one side's retaliatory forces could be dealt with by making provision to 'ride out' a nuclear exchange, and to have enough left over to retaliate. 'Intelligence' speculations, probably on both sides, always seem to show that the other side has more powerful forces than it really possesses. So it was that the 'bomber gaps' and the 'missile gaps' emerged—both spurious—to play so big a part in American politics. Those who set the pace in the arms-race—non-nuclear as well as nuclear—can always be relied upon to discover what have become known as 'windows of vulnerability'. Hence the continuing American debate about the likely vulnerability of the new MX nuclear system, even before it is deployed. The issue of the vulnerability of one's forces can always be made a challenge for the inventive genius of the men in the laboratories. Their simple answer to the challenge is to multiply those forces.

Another way is to develop effective defences, for example, anti-aircraft defences, and it was only natural that efforts would be made to devise corresponding defences against ballistic missiles. So, as the range and accuracy of missiles increased, the weaponeers started to impress on their service and political masters the need to defend missile sites, the argument being that unless it was certain that they were not vulnerable to attack, retaliatory nuclear forces would not be 'credible'. The Soviet Union and the United States were on the same tack. New weapon systems were therefore called for to satisfy the specifications of an anti-ballistic missile—ABM—scenario.

Both sides set about the job in the same way, just

as they deployed the same variety of anti-aircraft defences. There were 'acquisition radars' which scanned
the horizon for incoming warheads; 'tracking radars'
linked by computer to nuclear anti-missile missiles whose
explosion outside the atmosphere would emit x-rays to
which the attacking warheads would in theory be vulnerable at great distances; and then there were terminal
radars and terminal anti-missile missiles to deal with
such warheads as would not have been destroyed as
they sped though space. By the late sixties enough hardware and computer links had been developed to justify
deployment, or so it seemed.

But doubts had already started to set in.[5] Could
an ABM system work? It would have to deal not only
with nuclear warheads but with a variety of decoys and
other 'penetration aids' which the missiles would release
simultaneously in order to confuse the defensive radars.
Warheads might be exploded outside the atmosphere
to create an electromagnetic blackout that would make
the task of the radars almost impossible. The radars
themselves were clearly vulnerable to direct attack. The
scale of an attack could itself be so great as to swamp
any defensive system. Each ballistic missile could carry
not one but several warheads which, as was clearly
recognised as early as the mid-sixties, could be made
independently manoeuvrable—what we now call
MIRVed.[6] And then there was a political problem—
people did not want defensive nuclear missiles planted
in their backyards. Finally, neither the USA nor the
USSR could afford to deploy more than a handful of
defensive complexes. If these could be made to function

effectively, which was the first question that needed an answer, there was then a second problem, who or what was to be defended.

Despite all the doubts, in 1968 the United States Congress approved funds for the deployment of a 'light' ABM system, codenamed Sentinel (later cancelled by President Nixon), to defend against a hypothetical missile attack from China. The USSR had started a few years before to deploy one for the presumed defence of Moscow. For, as Mr Khrushchev saw it, if his ballisticians knew how to 'hit a fly in the sky', so too they could hit incoming warheads. It was therefore only rational to try to defend his capital city. President Johnson was not so sure. He was neither a physicist nor an engineer. In 1967 he asked a group of past and present presidential and top Pentagon science advisers the only question that mattered. Would an ABM system work or not? The answer from those best qualified to judge was 'no'.[7] No ABM system could reduce significantly the vulnerability of the United States; no President could initiate or agree to the initiation of a nuclear exchange without realising that once it had begun, he could never be sure where it would end—that the risk, were he ever to agree to the actual use of nuclear weapons, was the total devastation of his country. In 1967 President Johnson and Robert McNamara, his Defense Secretary, tried hard at Glassboro, New Jersey, to persuade Kosygin, Khrushchev's successor, to accept these propositions. Gradually he and the Politburo saw the light. Dubious ABM systems only destabilised a state of mutual nuclear deterrence.

The upshot was the ABM Treaty of 1972, when the two superpowers agreed to desist from the effort to deploy ABM systems in more than two (later changed to one) site each, but agreeing that ABM research and development could continue, subject to certain restraints.

But, paradoxically, the fruitless efforts to devise an ABM defence had resulted in the technological development of MIRVing, which almost at a stroke sharply increased the already enormous destructive potential of the armouries of the two sides. Given an ABM system could be devised, the technique had been developed in order to defeat the other side's defences. Action and reaction have always characterised the arms-race.

THE ARMS RACE

The quest for a defence against ballistic missiles has now taken new shape in President Reagan's Strategic Defense Initiative. Once again, technology is being given its head in seeking a solution to what is essentially a political problem.

The arms race is a race without a finishing post. There never can be an ultimate *military weapon*. What there can be is an ultimate *destructive agent*. Do we ask for more destructive power? Then the enemy 'hardens' his targets, or changes his tactics. Do we ask for another missile that is so designed that it can 'home' onto its target? Then the enemy alters the size of the target, or suppresses the tell-tale signals to which the sensors of the missile respond, or gives the target greater mobility. The process is circular. Each forward step necessitates the use of the latest scientific and technological developments. The easy steps have all been taken — only the most difficult remain. And these steps are, without exception, the most costly . . . so costly that the race increasingly distorts the pattern of a country's defence, even those of the richest countries.

Why then does the race go on? Let me suggest some reasons, but in no order of priority.

FIRST: The American and British air forces ended the second world war mesmerised by the idea that the more destruction they wreaked the better, and that the more the destruction that could be caused by a single bomb, still better. Here, now, was the answer: the atom bomb. It would dispose of all doubts that a country could be defeated in war by destroying its homeland. Reality would at last be accorded to the Douhet and Trenchard doctrines about strategic bombing.[8]

SECOND: During the brief period when only the USA had the bomb, a powerful sense was engendered that its very possession implied unchallengable military superiority. This sense has never faded—indeed it has spread, as those who are concerned about the effectiveness of the Non-Proliferation Treaty of 1968 fully recognise.

THIRD: In 1946 the United States Congress ruled that the responsibility for producing nuclear warheads was one for the civilian authority, not the military. For reasons of security, the scientists and engineers who design the nuclear warheads live in little communities cut off from the rest of the scientific world by dense veils of secrecy. They can discuss their work only with the few service people who are 'cleared' to talk to them. They usually put forward their own designs in accordance with their own perceptions, and then cast around for presumed military needs to which they can be related. Their outlook, even their scientific outlook, usually strays little further than the confines of the kind of science, mathematics and engineering that is needed to design a bomb or a ballistic missile. In the days when the Atomic Energy Commission was responsible for the work of the two weapons laboratories only a few of the handful of scientists who were involved were aware of what was going on in the political world outside the USA. Los Alamos and Livermore competed with each other in advancing new ideas. Even the people in the British weapons laboratory, established before Livermore, and who were allowed only a limited exchange with their US colleagues, enjoyed the competition.

FOURTH: As the years have passed, it has become more and more difficult for those full-time professionals who are involved in the design of new weapons to lift their heads above the nuclear mound they have created, and to cast their eyes over the political and military scene of which they are so small but dangerous a part.

FIFTH: There is always the fear that the Soviets might be on to something novel in the nuclear field. This acts as a spur to our own warhead zealots. Technology moves fast.

SIXTH: Interservice rivalry spurs the arms-race. It led the United States (and possibly at an early stage the USSR as well) to develop a triad of nuclear forces—

land-based, sea-based and air-based—which now makes it technically impossible for either side to disarm the other. Anti-submarine warfare has not yet reached the stage, if indeed it ever will, which makes even the small British or French nuclear-armed fleets vulnerable. But the technicians go on trying—and the nuclear arms-race continues.

SEVENTH: Few of our political and military leaders, who in the end are responsible for providing the resources for the pursuit of the nuclear trail, have time to reflect deeply about nuclear issues. They are conditioned into thinking that numbers of warheads matter, even when they acknowledge that we already have too many. They accept what they are told about the need to keep the nuclear deterrent 'credible', without realising that what matters is not what they think about the credibility of their own nuclear arsenals, but what they believe about the credibility of Soviet nuclear weapons—and, of course, *vice versa*. Never, in all my long experience of the nuclear problem, have I ever heard anyone suggest that because some Soviet nuclear bombs might be defective, we could risk a Soviet nuclear onslaught.

I hope that what I have said is enough to indicate why it is that no President, no Prime Minister, no Secretary of the Politburo, has yet cried 'halt' to his 'experts'. Not until one of them does will the nuclear arms-race cease. If a political leader is told that a series of tests must go on, he agrees without questioning. President Mitterrand of France has rejected all calls to stop nuclear tests in the Pacific with the legally correct observation that the tests are taking place on French territory, and that they will continue so long as they are necessary in the French national interest. But surely it was not the President himself who made the technical and military judgment that the tests are necessary to ensure French security? Unless it is the case that affairs in France are organised very differently from the way they are in the United Kingdom and in the United States, the judgment was in the main that of the experts in the French weapons laboratory. They, the technical experts, are the ones who at base decide these matters. Who advised President Reagan that the present series of American tests should continue? Clearly the authorities in Los Alamos, Livermore, and the Department of Energy. On what basis is the claim made that the Soviet Union is 'ahead', and that it is therefore necessary to go on testing? Ahead of what? We do not know what observations the Soviets were making in whatever tests they were carrying out underground before they stopped in the late summer of 1985, any more than they know about ours.

I have posed a few questions, and have indicated my own answers, because they are the answers I would have had to give had the questions been put to me when it was my responsibility to advise a succession of Prime Ministers on this subject.

Nuclear states opposed to each other cannot be expected to lower their guards, But nuclear technology, impelled by its own momentum, is no longer helping to increase, or even to safeguard, national security. Where do we go from here?

REFERENCES

1. Leonardo da Vinci, who lived in the last half of the fifteenth and beginning of the sixteenth centuries, is best remembered for his paintings and drawings. But as a renowned military engineer and scientist he also designed mortars, mines and catapults, and 'other machines of marvellous efficiency not in common use'.
2. Bernard O'Keefe, who gave this description (*The Nuclear Hostages*, Boston: Houghton Mifflin, 1983) was no stranger to nuclear tests. His experience with nuclear bombs began with the plutonium bomb which destroyed Nagasaki, and which it was Mr O'Keefe's responsibility to assemble. Subsequently, as a contractor, he was responsible for the coordination of several series of tests in the Nevada desert.
3. Liddell Hart, B. H., 1960, *Deterrent or Defence*, London: Stevens.
4. Evolution of Foreign Policy, speech to the Council on Foreign Relations, 12.1.54 (Department of State Press Release No. 8), quoted in Townsend Hoopes, 1974, *The Devil and John Foster Dulles*, London: Andre Deutsch.
5. See, for example, Ruina, J.P., and M. Gell-Mann, 1964, Ballistic Missile Defence and the Arms Race, *Proceedings of the Twelfth Pugwash Conference*, pp. 232–235.
6. See Garwin, Richard L., and Hans A. Bethe, 1968, Anti-ballistic missile systems, *Scientific American*, 218, 21–31.
7. York, Herbert F., 1970, *Race to Oblivion*, New York: Simon & Schuster.
8. The concept that wars can be won over the heads of battling armies by devastating the homeland of one's enemy with bombs was first elaborated by the Italian General Douhet and by the British Air Marshal Trenchard. In the United States it is associated with the name of General 'Billy' Mitchell.

3

Authority in a
Nuclear World

During the Second World War, before the nuclear age dawned, I had learnt at first hand about some aspects of military strategy and about the planning and measurement of destruction. But, like others, I had also learnt that in its execution, military strategy can distance itself from the political objectives it is designed to further and, more than that, that its outcome can be a new set of political realities which can be every bit as compelling and every bit as dangerous as those which brought the war about.

The totally unpredicted outcome of the war, and the reality with which it has stamped today's world—but with which we have not yet come to terms—is barely a reality at all, certainly not in any everyday sense. It is something so remote from all experience that we live with it without comprehension, sleeping soundly at night, occasionally, and then only vaguely, aware of words that warn that the arsenals of the United States and the USSR contain enough nuclear warheads to exterminate in one mighty flash a significant slice of humanity, including, in particular, all those who live in the cities of the northern half of the globe.

An associated reality is that the Western alliance is locked in a fierce ideological struggle with Moscow. The political objective of the West is to prevent the USSR from spreading the communist way of life, and so extending its sphere of influence beyond the vast areas which it now dominates. Equally Moscow is every bit as committed, not only to protecting its own way of life, and that of the wider political domain over which it rules, but also to continuing to promote its own relations, however often they are opposed to those of the West, with a post-colonial underdeveloped third world which is characterised by starvation and hardship, and torn by wars, revolutions, and counter-revolutions—not to mention terrorism.

More important for Europeans is the fact that the armed camps of East and West confront each other across a line which now divides the German nation into two, with mutual fear leading to the continuous build-up of armaments on both sides. The pace of the nuclear arms-race between the two sides has not yet been materially affected by the disarmament talks and negotiations that have been going on more or less uninterruptedly since the mid-fifties. In 1970, annual world military expenditure was estimated to be about $200 billion. In 1984, the corresponding figure was $800 billion.[1]

SUPERPOWER COMPETITION

Outside the realm of guerilla warfare, no military leader, however brilliant a strategist or tactician he might be, could expect to prevail over an able opponent who was significantly stronger in troops, guns, tanks, aircraft and warships. That the arms-race never slackens is therefore understandable in a world which is divided by fear and suspicion. It is a world where hatred pits one small nation against another—in the Middle and the Far East, in Africa, in the Caribbean, and in Central America—and with the main arms-producers supplying their 'client-states' with guns, tanks and aircraft and, for good measure, with anti-tank and anti-aircraft weapons as well.

At its start, the superpower competition in nuclear weaponry was presumably based on a mutually-held assumption that if it ever came to the crunch, one side could prevail over the other in a war in which nuclear arms were used. Correspondingly, it is the fear that there could be such a contest that now lies behind the widespread anti-nuclear movement in Europe: the fear that war might break out between the NATO alliance and the Warsaw Pact powers; that war in Europe could lead to the use of nuclear weapons; that once this happened the chances of such a war being contained are remote in the extreme; that neither side could win such a war; that both would be destroyed; and that all-out nuclear war could mean the end of western civilization, with tens and tens of millions dead within a matter of weeks, if not days.

Over the past twenty years these propositions have been proclaimed by an increasing number of men who have held the highest political and military office in both the Western alliance and the Warsaw Pact camps.

President Reagan was certainly not the first to declare that a nuclear war could not be won, and should therefore never be fought. The proposition is an implicit recognition that the Clausewitz doctrine—that war can be regarded as 'the continuation of political discourse with the addition of other means'—is nonsense when the 'other means' entail the risk of suicide. Nations—by which of course one means their leaders—do not embark on aggressive wars unless they believe that the chances of victory are greater than those of defeat.[2] Nor is it usual for them to resist the aggressor unless they believe that the cost of resistance is likely to be less than that of surrender.

But, regardless of these manifestly rational propositions, the two superpowers continue to behave as though they do not believe their own proclamations, that one *could* outbid the other in a nuclear contest, that there is meaning to the terms which characterise the nuclear debate, terms such as nuclear superiority or inferiority, of nuclear balance, or parity, or imbalance.

In reality, this kind of terminology is meaningless when considered against the immeasurably destructive power of the tens of thousands of nuclear weapons already in the arsenals of the NATO and Warsaw Pact powers. Indeed, they are dangerous anachronisms. Comparisons of numbers of tanks and aircraft make sense. Those of nuclear warheads no longer do. Nuclear weapons can be compared only in terms of the destruction they would cause. Once this is virtually total for both sides, the addition or subtraction of a thousand or so warheads on either side makes no difference at all to the basic realities.

The nuclear arms-race started in an atmosphere of hostility and suspicion, and it continues in suspicion. It began as soon as it became clear at the end of the Second World War that the USA, the USSR and the UK were not going to engage in any cooperative effort to develop 'the bomb' and, more particularly, when in 1946 the McMahon Act foreclosed any sharing by the United States of nuclear secrets with any other power. But regardless of Acts of Congress, there were no secrets about the facts of nuclear fission in the world of physics. The Soviet Union exploded its first test bomb in 1949, the year NATO was formed. The United Kingdom followed in 1952. France and China in turn became members of the nuclear-weapons club. Other countries might follow, mainly because of the belief that nuclear weapons have enormous military value. What other conclusion could non-nuclear states draw from the fact that nuclear armaments were shipped to American bases in Europe as soon as they became available, that one still hears that they have military utility, and that the two superpowers go on adding to their nuclear arsenals?

But weapons have military utility only so long as their effects can be predicted and, if used, when their consequences can be controlled. As weapons of war, nuclear weapons comply with neither condition. No one, as I have contended, knows how to control the destruction that would be caused by the incredible amounts of energy that are released in a nuclear explosion. Moreover, if one side were to initiate the use of nuclear weapons it could not expect to dictate the responses of its opponent, to whom the initiative would automatically pass. This is something that should never be forgotten. It is the basis for the view, recently endorsed by Robert McNamara, that the threat of a first use of nuclear weapons 'has lost all credibility as a deterrent to Soviet conventional aggression'. Their use, as he put it, 'would be an act of suicide', now that the USSR could in reply 'inflict unacceptable damage on Europe and the United States'.[3]

What all this boils down to is that while the threat of nuclear retaliation may deter a nuclear-armed enemy from taking hostile action, once used nuclear weapons do not provide any defence. Nor, as General Rogers, the present Supreme Commander of NATO forces has admitted,[4] is it possible to defend against nuclear weapons.[5]

Yet the nuclear competiton goes on, without either side adding to its security, and with both fearful that, through some technical miracle, its opponent might escape from the nuclear trap in which both are held captive. It is common ground that both already possess many times more nuclear weapons than are necessary to sustain a state of mutual deterrence. Both have proposed cuts of 50 percent in their nuclear armouries, and in my view either could do this unilaterally, eliminating whatever weapons it chose, without altering the real 'strategic' balance. But however irrational the thought may be, it would nonetheless be unrealistic to suppose that either of the superpowers would contemplate an unequal level of nuclear disarmament, one which could generate in its rulers a sense of insecurity.

INADVERTENT NUCLEAR 'WAR'

Time and time again the political leaders of the USA and the USSR have made declarations which boil down to the realisation that competition has become both a sterile and a perilous pursuit. They are wary of the danger of a nuclear exchange being started inadvertently. Incorrectly interpreted signals on radar screens have led to false alerts. False alerts have also been triggered in other ways. Mr McNamara has revealed that in 1962 the firing mechanisms could have operated when an American aircraft carrying nuclear bombs crashed on American soil. Had the firing mechanisms functioned, and a nuclear explosion had resulted, no one would have known whether American bombs or Soviet warheads had been the cause. When the news broke, a reassuring statement was issued saying that the bombs could never have gone off. That, however, is not the point. What mattered is what Mr McNamara and President Kennedy would have believed if the firing mechanisms had worked. If they had concluded that the Soviet Union had attacked, who knows whether or not they would have been driven to order a nuclear counter-attack?

The risk that a nuclear exchange could be precipitated by an aircraft of one side accidentally flying into the other's airspace is always there. This happened during the Cuban missile crisis when an American fighter-plane flew over Soviet territory in the far North-East. Khrushchev was informed of what had happened, but he ordered that the intruder should not be attacked.

He had enough trouble on his hands at the time without providing yet more fuel to the flames. The tragic affair in 1983 of the Korean civilian carrier KAL-007 is another example of what can happen. The aircraft, which had flown into 'sensitive' Soviet airspace and which had continued on its course after failing to respond to Soviet interceptors warning it to land, was shot down, killing its full load of passengers and crew, and with considerable international tension resulting.

A nuclear exchange could also start if a military leader were to take the law into his own hands. General LeMay, who was the Chief of America's Strategic Air Command in the late fifties, once said[6] that if he suspected that the Russians were mustering their bomber forces, he would carry out a pre-emptive strike on their airfields even if this were not Washington policy.[7]

In an article written in 1983,[8] Andrei Sakharov, the Soviet dissident physicist, expressed his anxiety that the great powers are drifting towards an all-out nuclear war. 'If', he wrote, 'the probability of such an outcome could be reduced at the cost of another ten or fifteen years of the arms race, then perhaps that price must be paid.' But ten years may well prove too long. Within that time a sixth or a seventh country could start manufacturing nuclear weapons and, despite the restraint that would be exercised by the superpowers, ignite a conflagration that could spread to the rest of the world. The 'mad' political leader, or independent general, or Dr Strangelove, who 'presses the button', need not be an American or a Russian, an Englishman or a Frenchman.

THE WEAPONRY OF POLITICS

As I have said, a country does not wittingly go to war unless there is a chance of winning, and it certainly would not do so if the likelihood were its utter destruction. If the day ever dawned when either of the superpowers deliberately fired a nuclear weapon, the act would be a test of political will. It would certainly not be an exercise of military wisdom. Nuclear warheads have become part of the weaponry of politics. They are stored in military armouries because these constitute the only convenient place where they can be held securely. There may have been moments of crisis when the thought of using nuclear weapons passed through the minds of political leaders, but, fortunately for mankind, their use has not been commanded since the last days of World War II.

The nuclear arms-race has not only brought about a nuclear stalemate. It has also forced both East and West into a mutual strategic vacuum, with the military commanders of neither side knowing how nuclear weapons could be used, and with their political masters fearful lest they are ever used. The vacuum has not been made less rarefied by those armchair strategists who, usually with little understanding of how armies operate or how human beings behave in war, describe with abandon scenarios of nuclear 'wars' in which millions of Americans and millions of Russians are wiped out. Nor has it been filled either by the directors of the weapons laboratories and their departmental and military sponsors, or by the boards of the industries that produce nuclear weaponry. Their business is to find ways of improving existing weapon systems, and to generate ideas for new ones.

The United Nations and its permanent Disarmament Committee have so far failed to make any meaningful impact on the nuclear arms-race. If it is ever to be curbed, it can be done only by the efforts of the two superpowers, working together. Only they, the political leaders of the two sides, have the authority and the power to slow down the race and bring it to an end. The potential cost of their failure to act more effectively than they have done so far is infinitely greater than the value of whatever compromises and sacrifices would be called for to reach agreement now.

In the mid-fifties the United States, the USSR, and the United Kingdom, then the only nuclear weapons states, got together to discuss a total ban on all further nuclear testing, and consequently a ban on the production of new types of nuclear warhead. After more than five years of detailed talks, the best that could be agreed was the Partial Test Ban Treaty of 1963. This left all parties free to pursue vigorous programmes of underground tests. A Non-Proliferation Treaty followed in 1968. There have been other treaties, of which the most important are: the first USA-USSR Strategic Arms Limitations Treaty (SALT I) and the ABM Treaty of 1972, and the SALT II Treaty of 1979—still not ratified by the American Senate. The important tripartite talks to agree on a comprehensive ban on testing that were started by President Carter in 1977 were allowed to lapse by President Reagan. The Geneva talks of 1982 to 1983, that were aimed at halting the deployment of Russian SS20 mobile nuclear missiles as well as the stationing on European soil of 572 American cruise and Pershing II missiles, were a failure. The United States has plans to introduce the MX and Trident II intercontinental systems, and also to deploy several thousand cruise missiles on ships and aircraft. The Russians are developing their own new systems, even though in the latter part of 1985 they unilaterally stopped underground testing. They have also declared that they are stopping the further deployment of SS20s. They have even gone further. Fewer than six months after the presumed failure of the Reykavik summit, they have unequivocally and unconditionally declared their willingness to accept the President's zero-zero offer that they rejected in 1983, so leading to the removal of all intermediate range ballistic missiles that are poised against each other in the European theater—all SS20s, Pershing IIs and cruise missiles. But equally they threaten to deploy more intercontinental types if work on the President's SDI is not brought to an end.

UNDERSTANDING AND COMMANDING NUCLEAR TECHNOLOGY

All nuclear weapons are 'strategic'—to use that sorely misused term. Were any NATO or Warsaw Pact nuclear weapon ever fired, the risks, as I have already emphasised, are that the conflagration would spread to an all-out exchange. SS20s, cruise and Pershing II missiles merely reflect the outcome of a process of technical change which adds little if anything to the threat that already exists.

The political leaders who were in power at the start of the nuclear age may perhaps be forgiven for not having appreciated that the weapons whose development they encouraged would inevitably transform the whole field of international relations. Clement Attlee, who in 1945 succeeded Winston Churchill as Prime Minister, records in his memoirs[9] that he then knew nothing 'about fall-out and all the rest of what emerged after Hiroshima. As far as I know,' he went on to say, 'President Truman and Winston Churchill knew nothing of these things either, nor did Sir John Anderson, who coordinated research on our side. Whether the scientists directly concerned knew, or guessed, I do not know. But if they did, then, so far as I am aware, they said nothing of it to those who had to make the decision.'

Roosevelt, Truman, Churchill and Attlee were not scientists. Attlee's confession of ignorance, as well as his question whether 'the scientists' knew, is nonetheless strange. He was certainly receiving advice from Patrick Blackett,[10] who, as a well-informed physicist as well as a man versed in military affairs, was very much aware of the risks. As Blackett put it, 'The dropping of the atomic bombs [on Hiroshima and Nagasaki] was not so much the last military act of the second world war, as the first act of a cold diplomatic war with Russia'.[11] Like a few other prominent British scientists, including Sir Henry Tizard,[12] he was highly dubious about the wisdom of the UK becoming a nuclear-weapons power. But their views did not prevail. A few months after Hiroshima, Attlee sanctioned the building of a pile to make fissionable material for atomic bombs.

Niels Bohr, a Dane and one of the greatest physicists of the day, had appreciated from the start the impact which the atom bomb would have on world politics. In October 1943, well before the fighting had ended, he was smuggled out of Denmark, and on his arrival in London, he had secret talks with the scientific and political leaders of the small British group that was concerned in the development of the bomb. He was then flown to the United States, where he visited Los Alamos and also conferred with a friend, Supreme Court Justice Felix Frankfurter, who happened to be an intimate of President Roosevelt. He then returned to London, where it had been arranged that he should see Winston Churchill, whom he tried, but unsuccessfully, to persuade that if the United States and the United Kingdom failed to tell the Russians about the work that was being done to produce a bomb, a nuclear arms-race would inevitably be triggered as soon as the fighting was over.[13] Winston Churchill was neither interested nor polite, and when at the end of the interview Bohr asked whether he could send Churchill a memorandum setting out the points he had made, Churchill is reported to have said, 'It will be an honour for me to receive a letter from you . . . but not about politics.'[14] Churchill's sole interest in the bomb at the time was what President Truman later called 'more bang for a buck'.

Bohr was flown back to Washington, where President Roosevelt is said to have listened to him carefully for over an hour. In a memo which Bohr sent the President after this visit, he pointed out that German and Russian, as well as American and British physicists, were informed about the facts of nuclear fission, and that it was necessary to bear in mind 'that the terrifying prospect of a future competition between nations about a weapon of such formidable character can only be avoided through a universal agreement in true confidence.'

He went on to say that:

> The prevention of a competition prepared in secrecy will therefore demand such concessions regarding exchange of information and openness about industrial efforts including military preparations as would hardly be conceivable unless at the same time all partners were assured of a compensating guarantee of common security against dangers of unprecedented acuteness. . . . Without impeding the importance of the project for immediate military objectives, an initiative, aiming at forestalling a fateful competition about the formidable weapon, should serve to uproot any cause of distrust between the powers on whose harmonious collaboration the fate of coming generations will depend.

In his illuminating analysis of the correspondence between President Roosevelt and Felix Frankfurter, Max Freedman summarises the issue in the following words:[15]

Continued secrecy would poison American-
Russian relations and endanger the prospects
for peace. Russia would have reason to think
that she had suffered a gigantic and unex-
ampled double-cross if the United States, while
talking of the partnership of war, worked in
unity with Britain but kept its entire atomic
program an absolute secret from the Soviet
Union. Perhaps a policy of disclosure would
not produce the open world. But the failure
to deal frankly with Russia would almost certainly produce a closed world, a world of division and discord, an armed world capable
for the first time in history of reducing itself
to a charred and poisonous rubble.

As is well known, Niels Bohr repeated and elaborated
all the arguments which he deployed with Winston
Churchill and F.D. Roosevelt in an open letter which
he addressed to the United Nations in 1950[16] He ended
his letter with a paragraph in which he said:

. . . every initiative from any side towards the
removal of obstacles for free mutual information and intercourse would be of the greatest importance in breaking the present deadlock
and encouraging others to take steps in the
same direction. The efforts of all supporters
of international co-operation, individuals as
well as nations, will be needed to create in
all countries an opinion to voice, with ever

increasing clarity and strength, the demand
for an open world.

Leo Szilard, the refugee Hungarian physicist who had
played a critical part in the development of the bomb,
also failed to get Niels Bohr's point appreciated by the
American authorities. James Franck, the Chicago physicist who, just before the testing of the first nuclear
warhead, was called upon to chair an official secret
committee on the social and political implications of
nuclear energy, fared no better. 'The race for nuclear
armaments', he warned, 'will be on in earnest not later
than the morning after our first demonstration of the
existence of nuclear weapons.'[17] There were also other
scientists who, before the first warhead had been tested,
realised that a weapon which at a stroke could eliminate
a great city was bound to cause a total break with the
strategic past, that it was bound to mark the beginning
of a new and dangerous stage in man's social evolution.

The few politicians and generals who knew about
the Manhattan Project to develop a bomb were not
interested in the political and strategic perceptions of a
few distinguished scientists. To them, the important
issue was the war, and if one casts one's mind back to
the anxieties of the time, it is difficult to imagine that
the decision to use the new weapon against Japan would
not have been taken. Moreover, to the Air Generals,
the atom bomb, given that it worked, would help justify
the concept of 'strategic air war'.

All that now lies in the past. What matters today
is that the enormous numbers of nuclear armaments

on both sides make 'nuclear accountancy', to use a term coined by Lord Carrington,[18] the present Secretary General of NATO, a meaningless exercise. Mutual extermination is not an acceptable way of dealing with political disputes. Moreover, whatever the way autocratic societies are ruled, the electoral processes of Western democracies surely do not confer on those who win power the right to 'press the button' as a sign of political determination, and so take the risk of exterminating their electoral opponents as well as their supporters.

When Lloyd George came up against the military machine during the first world war, he found that he 'had to contend not with a profession but with a priesthood devoted to a chosen idol'. The idol today, the popular symbol of military strength, is a nuclear warhead. In the public mind there has never been so powerful a symbol. How effective, one may well ask therefore, can the world's present political leaders be in controlling the idolatry that has been so successfully promoted by the nuclear priesthood which their predecessors of the post-war era encouraged so lavishly? I am not very optimistic.

THE FRUSTRATION OF POLITICAL AUTHORITY

Despite the fact that in the late fifties and early sixties not only Mr Macmillan, then the British Prime Minister, but also Presidents Eisenhower and Kennedy and, at first, even Khrushchev, were committed to achieving a comprehensive ban on the continued testing of nuclear warheads, they were successfully thwarted by most of the US and a few of the British scientists who were designing and testing warheads.

A basketful of reasons was offered to explain their opposition—in particular, the likelihood of cheating by the USSR, and the inadequacies of verification procedures. The considerable advances that had been made in the seismological techniques which make it possible to differentiate natural from man-made underground disturbances—that is to say, earthquakes from explosions—were not good enough for the scientists who opposed a ban. American, together with some British scientists, declared that the seismometers could not differentiate small explosions from natural rumbles in the earth's crust. Regardless of any treaty that they might have signed, the Russians, they argued, would take the risk of being caught cheating, even to test a warhead which could not make any difference to the strategic situation. As an official I had to take part in these discussions, and I used to ask, but in vain, when were we going to be satisfied with our seismological expertise—did we have to wait until we could differentiate the rumble of a truck or trucks from that made by a small charge of dynamite in a quarry? The argument that it is necessary to test stockpiled warheads for reliability, was also deployed, whenever necessary, as additional support for the claim that no nuclear power could live with a test ban. It was and still is both strategic and technical nonsense. Would either the USSR or the USA, already deterred by fears of nuclear retaliation, be any less deterred if they believed that a few warheads out of the thousands in their opponent's armoury were defective? And if in testing for reliability, a defective warhead were found, would one go on testing the rest to identify the duds, until there was nothing left in the stockpile?[19]

The men who were designing bombs wanted the right to pursue the course that was dictated by the technology. They did not regard it as their business to ask how relevant testing was to national security. Still eager for ever more destructive power, their military clients and supporters were only too ready to back the experts. Political pressure against a comprehensive ban built up fast, and, as I have said, a partial Test-Ban Treaty was the most that could be achieved.

When, towards the end of his presidency, Eisenhower became concerned about the inordinate demands for new weapon systems made by the United States Strategic Air Command (SAC), he sent the late George Kistiakowsky, his Science Adviser, and two of the latter's colleagues (one of them the scientific Deputy Director of the CIA) to SAC's headquarters in Omaha to see what was afoot.[20] They searched SAC's targeting list to find a Soviet town which corresponded in size to Hiroshima, the city that had been utterly destroyed by a warhead with a yield of some 14 kt. One was found, and it turned out that the Omaha targeteers had 'allocated' to it a 4.5 *megaton* warhead, to be followed if needs be by three with a yield of one-megaton—a total yield about half a million times more than it took to efface Hiroshima! This still goes on—on both sides. The public is today being deluded by those who pretend that there is some kind of scientific justification for the abracadabra practised by Western and Soviet nuclear theorists.

In my first chapter I argued that the long-term social and political—and, I would now add, military —consequences of major technological innovations are not usually predictable. They are no more predictable than are the predictions of economists who, ostensibly working on the same basis of impartial fact, but not necessarily committed to the same political philosophy, offer widely divergent recipes for the management of the economy, whether in the free societies of the West or the dirigiste ones of the communist world. Gunnar Myrdal, a distinguished Swedish economist and Nobel Laureate, once said that there are no disinterested social scientists; that before economists offer their prescriptions they should declare their 'value judgments', and not conceal them as implied assumptions; that they should stand up and be counted for their political beliefs. Those applied defence scientists and technologists who promote their wares in the defence field, and who also do not know exactly how they will turn out, or what strategic impact they are likely to have, should also stand up and be counted. By taking the lead in major weapon developments they are usurping the constitutional responsibility of Chiefs of Staff as advisers to Presidents or Prime Ministers on matters of national security. Non-scientific politicians cannot be expected to differentiate scientific advice that is coloured by obsession or political prejudice from dispassionate advice. It becomes all the more dangerous when the prejudices—American or Russian—are those which fan the fears and suspicions which now divide the two superpowers.

To conclude—the continuing competition in nuclear arms between East and West is a political matter. It no longer has whatever little military significance it may once have possessed. Theatre nuclear forces became an issue, not because they were needed, but because of a presumed political fear that, if it ever came to the crunch, America might desert her European allies, and in the hope that this would not happen if a new generation of American missiles were deployed on European soil. Equally blind, the USSR failed to recognise that the NATO command regarded the deployment of SS20s as constituting an additional and more dangerous threat than that posed by the SS4s and SS5s which they were going to replace, despite the fact that from any rational point of view, the Soviet weapons already targeted against Western Europe were already a total threat. In the context of the 'numbers game', the USSR was being no more than logical when they viewed with increasing alarm the Pershing IIs and cruise missiles which were to be deployed in Europe, even when, in theory, these were only a trivial addition to a vast array of ICBMs and to the several thousand cruise missiles which the United States proposes to deploy on its own ships and aircraft. Clearly the USSR also views the warheads in the British and French armouries, whether labelled strategic or theatre or tactical, as part of the cumulative threat which they face on the European mainland. In the context of nuclear accountancy, we would certainly treat Czech or Polish or East

German nuclear armaments—given they had them and however they were styled—as an additional strategic threat from the Warsaw Pact, regardless of the fact that a small fraction of what the USSR already has targeted against us could destroy us utterly.

A remarkable letter that was penned by President Eisenhower in 1956[21] has recently come to light. He began by saying that he had spent his life 'in the study of military strength as a deterrent to war, and in the character of military armaments necessary to win a war'. He then went on:

> we are rapidly getting to the point that no war can be *won*. War implies a contest; when you get to the point that contest is no longer involved and the outlook comes close to destruction of the enemy and suicide for ourselves . . . then arguments as to the exact amount of available strength as compared to somebody else's are no longer the vital issues.

And he concluded:

> When we get to the point, as we one day will, that both sides know that in any outbreak of general hostilities, regardless of the element of surprise, destruction will be both reciprocal and complete, *possibly we will have sense enough to meet at the conference table with the understanding that the era of armaments has ended and the human race must conform its actions to this truth or die.* [author's italics]

That is the reality of our nuclear world.

That is the reality with which authority now has to wrestle.

That is the background against which SDI has to be considered.

REFERENCES

1. *SIPRI Yearbook*, 1985, London & Philadelphia: Taylor & Francis.
2. As Lloyd George, Britain's leader in World War I, put it, 'All nations alike enter into a war with an equal confidence in ultimate victory for their banners. Defeat is always a surprise to the vanquished' (*War Memoirs*, 1, London: Odhams, 1938, p. ix).
3. McNamara, Robert S. (Fall 1983), *Foreign Affairs*, 59–80.
4. Quoted in Peter Nichols, 1983, 'The general a long way from Apocalypse Now,' *The Times* (March 12).
5. This point was made in 1940 by R. E. Peierls and O. R. Frisch, in the brief in which they outlined for the first time how to make an atomic bomb (see Gowing, Margaret, 1964, *Britain and Atomic Energy*, London: Macmillan).
6. Kaplan, Fred, 1983, *The Wizards of Armageddon*, New York: Simon & Schuster, p. 134. *and* LeMay, Curtis E., with Dale O. Smith, 1968, *America is in Danger*, New York: Funk & Wagnalls, p. 83.
7. The U2 intelligence flights over the Soviet Union were the responsibility of the CIA. President Eisenhower is said to have been completely confused about the facts of the ill-fated sortie by Gary Powers in 1960 until confronted with them by Khrushchev.
8. Sakharov, A., 1983, *Foreign Affairs*, 61, 1010.
9. Williams, Francis, 1961, *A Prime Minister Remembers*, London: Heinemann.

10. Later Lord Blackett, a Nobel Laureate in physics, and President of the Royal Society.

11. Blackett, Patrick M. S., 1948, *Military and Political Consequences of Atomic Energy*, London: Turnstile Press.

12. Sir Henry Tizard, FRS, was a physicist who before the Second World War was Secretary of the Government's Department of Scientific and Industrial Research and Rector of Imperial College. He then became chairman of the Government's Scientific Survey of Air Defence and Scientific Adviser to the Chief of the Air Staff. In 1942 he became President of Magdalen College, Oxford, and in 1946, Chairman of both the Government's Defence Research Policy Committee and Advisory Council on Scientific Policy.

13. In 1941, three years before Bohr's abortive visits, Peter Kapitza, the distinguished Soviet physicist who had been one of Lord Rutherford's famous team working on nuclear physics in the Cavendish Laboratory, had published in *Izvestia* (13 October, 1941), and with the authority of the Soviet leadership, a statement in which he appealed for a cooperative effort in the development of the bomb. Kramish, A., 1960, *Atomic Energy in the Soviet Union*, London: OUP.

14. Gowing, Margaret, 1964, *Britain and Atomic Energy*, London: Macmillan, pp. 354–55, and Moore, Ruth, 1967, *Niels Bohr*, London: Hodder & Stoughton, pp. 342–43.

15. Freedman, Max, 1968, *Roosevelt and Frankfurter; Their Correspondence 1928–1945*, London: The Bodley Head, pp. 733–34, 726.

16. Bohr, Niels, 1950, *Open Letter to the United Nations*, Copenhagen: Schultz.

17. *Bulletin of the Atomic Scientists*, 1946, 1 (10).

18. Alastair Buchan Memorial Lecture, given at the Institute for Strategic Studies, London, April 1983.

19. Some of the more prominent of those civilian scientists who carried the responsibility for warhead reliability in

the USA have recently put themselves on public record that 'In no case was the discovery of a reliability problem dependent on a nuclear test and in no case would it have been necessary to conduct a nuclear test to remedy the problem.' Such testing 'would be completely impractical' (Letter from Hans Bethe, Norris Bradbury, Richard Garwin, Spurgeon M. Keeny, Jr., Wolfgang Panofsky, George Rathjens, Herbert Scoville, Jr., and Paul Warnke, to the Chairman of the Committee on Foreign Affairs, 14 May 1985). The argument was simply one of several debating points to encourage innocent politicians to oppose a comprehensive ban on tests, whatever the circumstances. It is an unfortunate fact that all these arguments were seized upon by the Soviet nuclear enthusiasts who, while silent in the public debate, were as keen to go on testing as were their opposite numbers on the Western side. Inordinate and unreal demands about verification play very nicely into Soviet hands.

20. Kaplan, Fred, 1983, *The Wizards of Armageddon*, New York: Simon & Schuster, p. 269.

21. Letter, Dwight D. Eisenhower to Richard L. Simon, 4 April 1956 (Dwight D. Eisenhower Library, Abilene, Kansas). Also quoted in the *Washington Post*, 7 September, 1983.

4

The Wonders of
Star Wars

The November, 1985 Geneva summit has come and
gone, as has Reykavik, of October, 1986, and Mr Gorbachev is still adamant that the full Strategic Defense
Initiative programme is a critical impediment to any
significant arms control agreement in the strategic
sphere—for the simple reason that it would inevitably
drive the arms race into space. President Reagan on
the other hand, remains bewitched by what he continues to call his dream, a dream of a shield of defence
systems in space which would liberate mankind from
'the prison of mutual terror'. So there it is—as the
USSR sees it, a choice between survival and mutual
suicide; for Mr Reagan, a beautiful dream. Where does
reason lie? Will there be anything new at the next
summit?

Had anyone other than the American President
ever invited scientists to try to render 'nuclear weapons
impotent and obsolete', the suggestion would probably
have attracted no more attention than had they been

asked to square the circle or solve the problem of perpetual motion. But it happened to be the President, and he spelled out his vision of a future over which the nuclear bomb no longer casts a shadow in such homely terms that it all sounded real. How could the message fail to appeal? There was also a promise of vast resources for R&D—a vision therefore not only of peace but, at least in the meantime, of work, prosperity, and excitement for some. For those who might object that the idea was strategically naive, the President even acknowledged that it would 'take years, probably decades of effort' for the dream to become a reality, and that in the meantime defensive systems, 'if paired with offensive systems,' could be 'viewed as fostering an aggressive policy.'[1] However fantastic it was, the challenge therefore had to be taken seriously, even by the President's Defense Secretary who, it had been widely rumoured, had been sceptical about the idea until the moment it was suddenly proclaimed to the world.

The upshot is that within the space of three years, SDI has become one of the best-known acronyms in the world. It has stimulated a global debate. Instead of reducing tensions between East and West and 'introducing greater stability into the strategic calculus of both sides,' it has exacerbated the tensions. It has also generated strains in the Western alliance. Even more important, it has divided that part of the American scientific community to which the challenge was particularly addressed, with respect both to its technological implications and to its strategic desirability—a part of the debate in which politicians, military people, and ordinary citizens have also engaged. And of course the debate has produced a mountain of comment.

In some respects the debate is a re-run of the controversies that culminated in the 1972 ABM Treaty discussed in Chapter Two, when both sides implicitly acknowledged that it was then beyond their power to design meaningful defences against intercontinental ballistic missiles. But this time it was not a case of an American President trying to persuade the political head of the USSR to desist from pursuing a fruitless search for security. It was the other way round, with Mr Gorbachev, Kosygin's successor, trying to persuade Reagan, Johnson's successor, that his SDI is a dangerous dream.

The 1972 ABM Treaty did not bar development work that improved the radars, computers, and defensive missiles deployed within the two sites allowed, but specifically prohibited the development of any type of space-based ABM system. Stability was then the order of the political day.

And that was the moment—not March of 1983 when President Reagan spoke—when SDI really began. For, not surprisingly, the American and Soviet scientists and engineers who had been working on lasers and particle beams as possible Ballistic Missile Defence (BMD) weapons did not cease their experimental inquiries when the 1972 treaty was signed, any more than did the scientists and engineers who were trying to improve the power of the permitted radars and computers, and the design, thrust, and speed of their defending missiles. The military chiefs on both sides, who had anyhow been dubious about the wisdom of the ABM

Treaty, were only too ready to encourage them to continue, however little they understood the intricacies of the systems concerned. Most of the scientists and engineers needed little urging. After all, it was their jobs that were on the line.

An important figure who was in no need of any encouragement was Edward Teller, the well-known refugee theoretical nuclear physicist who had worked on the atom bomb under Hans Bethe during the war years. Teller is regarded by some as a distinguished, by others as a notorious, physicist. During the McCarthy years he had played a critical part in the downfall of Robert Oppenheimer, the wartime scientific director of Los Alamos, whether because of jealousy and frustration or because he had conceived of himself as some kind of super-patriot—*plus royal que le Roi*—it was difficult to say.

Whatever his motives, Teller lost the respect of most of his scientific peers, from whom he rapidly became isolated.[2] On the other hand he was eagerly supported by members of the defence establishment, particularly in the Air Force, who were only too ready to agree that a more powerful nuclear device than the atom bomb, the 'second generation' hydrogen bomb, would be a valuable addition to America's nuclear arsenal.

They also supported him in his campaign to found a second nuclear warhead laboratory at Livermore as an offshoot of the University of California. Teller had persuaded them that the Los Alamos research centre was too liberal. He vehemently opposed the Partial Test

Ban Treaty of 1963, basically because it interfered with the testing of new warhead designs, but protesting too that the Soviet Union would be bound to cheat—and that anyhow there was no reason to suppose that the radioactive fallout from nuclear tests in the atmosphere did any harm, it might even do good.[3] He became the chosen scientific mouthpiece of the 'hard-line right', a term that Europeans have come to identify with those Americans who are intrinsically against arms control, who uncritically assume that more destructive nuclear power than what already exists means more military and political strength, and who, whatever the risks, wish to oppose the Russians and communism at all times and wherever possible.

Teller was also loud in his protestations against the ABM Treaty and against SALT I and II. The Livermore laboratory, his creation, was going to give birth to a third-generation nuclear device that would transform the entire strategic scene. According to William Broad, the author of a book called *Star Warriors*,[4] the picture of this third generation of nuclear devices that Teller painted for the President was largely instrumental in instilling in Mr Reagan's mind a vision of a future in which nuclear weapons could be made impotent and obsolete.

Teller thus lurks behind almost every page of Mr Broad's book, which focuses on a small but select group of the employees of Livermore, who now number, so we are told, some eight thousand, and who cost the Federal government more than $800 million a year: Although Livermore does many other things, its primary function is the design of warheads, a field in which it competes fiercely, and presumably very successfully, with the older Los Alamos laboratory. A glossy brochure that was issued to celebrate the station's silver anniversary claimed that Livermore was responsible for nine of the ten strategic warheads now in the American nuclear stockpile. As Mr Broad was told by a member of the special group with whom he spent a week in the Livermore compound, warhead and weapon designers are free to follow their heads—the number of possible designs is 'limited only by one's creativity'. The young men Mr Broad was getting to know were the ones who were responsible for Teller's third-generation nuclear breakthrough.

Their leader, and Teller's main disciple, is Dr Lowell Wood, who is in his early forties. For a week Mr Broad stayed with him, consorting during all hours of the day and night with his host's team, which was designated O Group at Livermore, and which numbered no more than a dozen or so young scientists of average age less than thirty. Associated with them were as many part-time workers, some of whom were no more than graduate students. Many of the team had begun as research fellows of the Hertz Foundation, on whose board both Teller and Wood sat, and for which Wood served as the recruiting sergeant. With employment prospects bleak, and competition for jobs fierce, he was able to select from all the universities of the US young scientists and engineers in whom he discerned 'outstanding capability that has been developed and exercised in some direction'—usually in mathematics or physics. Apparently men with general interests but no specialized technical accomplishment were not wanted.

Successful candidates were invited to work at Livermore for a summer in an intern programme, and were kept on if they made the grade. All but a few of the group were, like Wood himself, bachelors. Few had set out to be bomb makers; but it was either that or, as one of the group told Mr Broad, working in a 'beet cannery'. There was the further attraction that Livermore had the most marvellous equipment with which to work, as well as access to the underground nuclear testing grounds of Nevada, which were shared—in effect as an outstation—with Los Alamos and the Sandia nuclear development establishment at Albuquerque.

Lowell Wood's young men both collaborated and competed with one another, and celebrated their triumphs at parties at which they ate masses of ice cream and drank gallons of Coca-Cola. Mr Broad tells us that there were no women around and that O Group was not entirely popular in the main Livermore establishment, one member of which told Mr Broad that the team was made up of 'bright young hotshots' with 'no outside interests . . . who are socially maladjusted'.

If the week that Mr Broad spent with the hotshots was typical, they also seemed to converse only with one another, and when not discussing their work, exchanged naive views about politics. One would imagine from the conversations Mr Broad describes that the only problem in the world for O Group is the competition for power between the USSR and the US. Their part of the problem was to construct a shield to keep out Soviet warheads. One of the group told Mr Broad that as soon as that was done, the US would leave the USSR technologically 'in the dust', and that success would 'prove to the world that democracy works'. Another told him that if the Russians 'owned the planet' they would not allow the evolution of technology to continue. So far as this young man knew, 'the only reason they are going with technology is that they can't afford not to.' He clearly was unaware that in the 1930s the USSR had shocked the West with a revelation of a totally utilitarian view of science and of its absolute commitment to technology.[5] The revelation would have appealed to Lowell Wood and his team, for they are doers, not philosophers or political scientists. Their business, like that of their opposite numbers in the USSR, is to put scientific knowledge to work.

LIVERMORE

Long before any of them was born, long before the era of ICBMs, physicists had been building machines—for example, cyclotrons and proton synchrotons—in which the subatomic particles that make up the atom are accelerated into extremely powerful beams of energy. These 'particle beams', if directed into space, might, it was later thought, intercept and destroy nuclear warheads. Then, in 1960, came the laser. Ordinary light, as emitted by the heated filament of a light bulb, consists of an incoherent emission of a very wide band of electromagnetic waves—from the longer ones at the red end of the visual spectrum to the shorter ones at the blue. The laser focuses all the energy of a very narrow band of the electromagnetic spectrum within a coherent beam or jet. The discovery[6] was seized upon by scientists the world over for a myriad of different purposes, from an instrument that can be used for operations on the retina of the eye, to an aiming device for marksmen.

It was not surprising that 'defence scientists' also saw in the laser, as in the particle beam, a device which, if furnished with sufficient energy, could operate at great distance—the sort of thing an older generation would have called a death ray. Retired generals started to talk about particle beams as though they were particles which could be poured from one hand to another. The newspapers were not slow to hint at a new generation of wonderful weapons.

The main achievement of O Group, and in particular of Peter Hagelstein, whom Mr Broad introduces to his readers as the brightest star of Lowell Wood's team and as a young and troubled engineer who is also interested in classical music and French literature, was the presumed invention of the 'nuclear-pumped' X-ray laser. Other workers, including an older Livermore scientist, had already bent their talents to this problem, but in vain. X-rays belong to the extreme shortwave end of the electromagnetic spectrum (about one thousandth the wavelength of visible light). If a coherent beam of X-rays could be provided with sufficient energy, it would travel outside the atmosphere at the speed of light for thousands of kilometres, imparting its energy to the 'first fraction of a millimeter of the aluminum skin of a missile [in its path]. This paper-thin layer would explode, sending a shockwave ['thump'] through the missile,' so destroying it.[7] This is the concept that was Teller's basic justification for believing that a space-based ABM system was a possibility. A sufficiently powerful X-ray or other laser or particle beam travelling at the speed of light, that is to say at 186,300 miles a second, could, if properly aimed, destroy a warhead whose maximum speed was less than ten miles a second.

Were an X-ray laser to serve as an ABM weapon, it would, however, be necessary to use as a source or 'pump' of energy a nuclear device, i.e., bomb, of significant force (maybe 100 kilotons in yield or more). On the other hand, in theory the X-ray laser is not the only laser that could do the trick. Los Alamos, among other laboratories, is working on an 'excimer' or chemical laser whose wavelength, although much longer than those of X-rays, would be equally effective (but by heating, not 'thumping', the target), without the disadvantage that X-rays could be made to lase only at the enormous temperatures associated with the explosion of a nuclear weapon.

Since X-rays are absorbed by even a thin layer of the atmosphere, another disadvantage of the nuclear-pumped X-ray laser is that it is a device which in practice could only be effectively fired when shot up into space, or shot from a space satellite, a so-called space battle station—which indeed would be necessary for most subatomic particle-beam weapons. An X-ray space battle station would, of course, be a one-shot device, since the whole thing would be destroyed an infinitesimal fraction of a second after the nuclear explosion that generates X-rays, which would be directed along, and amplified by, a series of lasing metal rods built around the whole device. Given certain conditions, the rods could in theory be independently aimed in that millionth of a second at a number of enemy launchers as they rose from their silos.

Only land-based weaponry was involved in the ABM systems with which the 1972 agreement was concerned. There was no possibility then of hitting ballistic missiles during their launch phase; since decoys and other countermeasures ruled out effective interception in space, warheads would have become vulnerable only when they re-entered the atmosphere on the way to their automatically designated targets.

The 1983 system, if SDI can be called that, differs completely because it is a space-based concept. The theory is that beam weapons or rocket fire could be directed from artificial satellites against enemy missiles during the few minutes of their launch phase, before the ejection of their multiple warheads, and thousands of miles from the targets which they would be programmed to destroy. The same arguments would apply to the electromagnetic rail-gun, another device now being worked on, which uses intense magnetic fields to create the force to shoot out small projectiles ('smart rocks') at very high velocity.

Were it ever possible to bring laser, particle-beam,

or electromagnetic rail-gun weapons into action during this initial phase of the flight of a missile, the defensive system would also have to include enough artificial surveillance satellites to ensure that as they circled the globe, there would at all times be at least one that was looking down on the Soviet missile fields. Otherwise the curvature of the earth would make it impossible for one or the other side to see its opponent's missiles before their warheads were well into space. The weapons on the 'battle stations' circling the earth would have to be ready to be aimed and to strike on automatic command.

But here lies the first major problem. Teller, who we have been led to believe started the whole thing, is convinced that battle stations permanently in space are too vulnerable to enemy attack to be contemplated. Even if, as Lowell Wood suggested to Mr Broad, they were placed in geosynchronous orbit more than 20,000 miles above the earth, they could in theory be 'fooled'—for example, by decoy launches on the ground or by decoys in space furnished with transmitters to send out false signals to confuse the BMD sensor systems.[8] Or they could also be destroyed by space mines, small satellites that would follow the battle stations and would always be ready to explode.

Space-based attacking systems also suffer from an additional handicap—the power sources by which they would be activated would be both very heavy and very bulky. Teller's view is that the X-ray laser, his favourite weapon, should be carried in submarines, and launched into space—'popped-up' is the happy-go-lucky term that is used—by ballistic missiles which would react automatically when commanded to do so by the surveillance satellites that registered the Soviet SS18 and other missiles rising from their silos or launch pads.

Once shot into space, the X-ray laser devices would automatically be focused onto the presumably unprotected boosters, which, as they rose above the atmosphere, would be 'thumped' by an X-ray laser beam set off by the explosion of a hydrogen bomb. Excimer or chemical lasers on the ground might in theory reach their targets by way of a system of folded mirrors that would be orbiting the earth, ready to open up on computer command to reveal themselves as perfect large reflecting surfaces. These would change their orientation in split second after split second as they aimed the beams impinging on them either directly to their targets, or redirected them to other mirrors that would do the focusing.

Then there would be a computer network that would tie all the surveillance satellites, targeting devices, beam and ray weapons into a single system competent to deal not with one or a few enemy missiles but, if the space shield were to be truly impregnable, with hundreds, even thousands.

What all this means is that if it ever came to action, heaven would become hell within a few minutes, and, given a failure of the system, that hell would also break out on earth in less than an hour. What is more, even though the whole system would have to start reacting automatically at a moment's notice, somehow or other—no one has said how—there would have to be time for a human link in the chain of interacting processes. As a sop to the the doubters, the proponents of SDI agree that the fate of mankind is not something that should be simply committed to a computer.

Teller, Lowell Wood and his whiz-kids, as well as their opposite numbers in Los Alamos and such supporters as they have in the Pentagon and the Department of Energy, believe that all this can be done, or at least that it is worth spending tens of billions of dollars to see whether it can be done. Little time passed, however, before it became clear that some members of Congress had doubts, and that the views of the space warriors were not shared by a number of scientists who know about these things, both within and outside government laboratories. Lowell Wood asserts that all the opposition emanates from a very few scientists. At a small international meeting, not mentioned by Mr Broad in his fascinating book, Wood told his audience that the number of scientific sceptics could be counted on the fingers of one hand. Unfortunately he said on the fingers of a *maimed* hand, which rather shocked his audience and reduced the force of his argument.

PROPONENTS AND CRITICS

In fact, the situation is the reverse of what Lowell Wood believes. According to Dr John Bardeen, twice a Nobel Prize winner in physics, there are few scientists either within or outside the administration who believe that President Reagan's dream could be realized in the foreseeable future. Dr Bardeen was a member of the White House Science Council at the time of Mr Reagan's SDI speech, about which both the Council and Dr George Keyworth, its chairman, were ignorant until five days before it was delivered.[9] Nor does Teller share Lowell Wood's views about the number of scientific doubters. He told Mr Broad that 'a great many American scientists, perhaps the majority,' are against SDI. The fact is that only a very few independent scientists have come forward to offer their support to the Livermore and Los Alamos enthusiasts. Of these, the quickest off the mark was Dr Robert Jastrow, a well-known popularizer of science, and a professor of earth sciences at Dartmouth College. His unswerving loyalty to SDI shines out in *How to Make Nuclear Weapons Obsolete*.[10]

Dr Jastrow's short book begins with a number of fairly unassailable propositions. Defence, he tells us, is always a good thing; a policy of mutual nuclear deterrence is inhumane since it implies a willingness to destroy populations; if one side acquired an effective defence against ballistic missiles, it could attack the other with impunity; if both had a defence, nuclear arms would become useless; even an imperfect US defence that left some of its retaliatory weapons untouched would foreclose the possibility of a first strike by the USSR. Why the USSR should in any circumstances want to risk such a strike, knowing that the considerable submarine missile fleet of the United States would be immune to attack, Dr Jastrow does not make clear. As former President Nixon has recently reminded us, the Soviet leaders are neither madmen nor fools.[11]

Dr Jastrow then gives an account of the build-up of Soviet land-based missiles in the years since the signing of the SALT treaties, implying that doing so was contrary to what the treaties allowed. For Dr Jastrow, the USSR has only one end in view, namely the destruction of the land-based components of the US nuclear arsenal in a first strike. Here Dr Jastrow's echo of the conventional Pentagon view again clashes with the position of Nixon, who in his *Foreign Affairs* article observes that the Russians have gained whatever 'superiority' they have 'in strategic land-based missiles not because of what *they* did in violation of arms control agreements but because of what *we* [the US] did *not* do within the limits allowed by the agreements.'

Dr Jastrow writes about the airborne and submarine elements of the US nuclear arsenal, including the Trident missile, in terms that rather belittle their value. He talks mysteriously of work going on which will make it possible to detect deeply submerged submarines. This is a possibility that has been continuously discussed and explored over the years, but so far with no results that would undermine the view that nuclear submarines are, and will continue to be, effectively invulnerable. The picture Jastrow paints seems to imply that America is wide open to attack by the more powerful armoury of the USSR. The only real hope, therefore, is 'a defense that shielded the American people'. And despite what the critics say, that, he asserts, is already available. The new secret weapon is the 670-million-mph laser beam. With this introduction Dr Jastrow takes us back to SDI.

It turns out that he was so inspired by the President's speech of March 1983 that he immediately and publicly gave it his scientific imprimatur. He then became fortified in his faith by a talk given by Dr Keyworth, who, in the earlier years of the Presidency, was Mr Reagan's science adviser and who, Mr Broad tells us, was recommended to the President by Teller. Dr Keyworth, a former member of the staff of Los Alamos, outside which he was little known before, is a friend of Teller. It would have been surprising if he had not been an ardent crusader for space defence.[12]

Much of the material for Dr Jastrow's book was provided by Gregory Canavan of Los Alamos, and by Lowell Wood of Livermore, by General James A. Abrahamson, the head of the Pentagon's SDI office, and by a few other officials whom he names. The book contains no original analysis, which perhaps is not surprising since it would seem that Dr Jastrow has not himself been involved in research either on nuclear weapons or on lasers, radars, or computers. He is a missionary for SDI.[13] What the reader therefore gets is a highly optimistic account of the same hypothetical space defensive system of which countless descriptions have already been published.

Can 'inventive genius', Dr Jastrow asks, find a device that can shield the American people? Of course it can. The invention is already there. 'It is called the laser'. And the way Dr Jastrow writes makes it all but child's play to fit together the whole defensive complex. The US could deploy a Mark I system by the early 1990s[14] and all for a cost of $60 billion, for which could be bought one hundred satellites, each carrying 150 interceptor rockets, four early-warning satellites in geosynchronous orbits, lower altitude satellites for surveillance, acquisition, tracking, and terminal defence, all the necessary but as yet non-existent computer networks and other accessories. Everything can be 'easily' achieved. Terms such as 'easy' and 'not too difficult' characterize Dr Jastrow's rosy picture.

His optimism is matched only by his breathtaking simplifications. War in space—that is to say, intercepting nuclear warheads with laser or particle beams or with pellets shot from electromagnetically driven rail-guns—is for him like an infantry battle. If the battle-management satellite loses touch with its weapons satellites, they can function autonomously—'like a machine-gunner cut off from his unit'. It would, however, be better, so he writes, were they under the control of the master satellite which, like the general in charge of a land battle, can oversee the whole operation, moving his forces as required. The control function would be exercised by a master satellite—not, it should be noted, by the President of the United States in consultation with the heads of NATO governments—during the three to five minutes of the boost phase of the enemy missiles, whose targets this time would not be hostile soldiers, but defenceless cities with millions of inhabitants in peril of instant death. It reads like a film script. I suspect that were Dr Jastrow's book to be made required reading for the leaders of America's NATO allies, what reluctant political support some of them have been prevailed upon to give to President Reagan's dream would vanish overnight.

Dr Jastrow fully realizes that a large number of highly reputable American scientists regard the entire idea as technical and strategic nonsense. Yet almost the only point of criticism on which he concentrates relates, first, to an erroneous early estimate, in a report by scientists opposed to SDI, of the number of surveillance satellites that would have to orbit the earth in order to keep the Soviet missile fields constantly in view, and, second, to an estimate of the considerable weight of a satellite that would be demanded by a particle-beam weapon. Dr Jastrow did not himself spot the errors. He says he learned about them when they were rumoured by 'professionals in the field'. In fact the authors of the report in question,[15] which included such distinguished scientists as Hans Bethe, Richard Garwin, Victor Weisskopf, Kurt Gottfried, and Henry Kendall, themselves drew public attention to the two errors five weeks after their report was issued, and before anyone else had done so.[16]

They also made quite sure that their subsequent publications were free of computational errors, at the same time emphasizing that estimates of the numbers of surveillance and laser satellites that a defensive system might call for depended on a varying number of assumptions. Dr Garwin has subsequently published what seems to be the most complete and unchallenged set of estimates, given several different assumptions.[17] At any rate it is judged as such by Edward T. Gerry,[18] the chairman of the relevant panel of the Pentagon's Fletcher study team,[19] which the administration set up in 1983 to advise whether the pursuit of a space-based defensive system was technically justifiable.

In reality the two computational errors did not

affect any substantive judgment about the feasibility of a space-based defence, as emerged clearly from a vigorous and lengthy exchange of letters published in *Commentary* in March 1985. Dr Jastrow, who took part in the exchange, nonetheless again hammered away at the errors in an article published later in the summer,[20] in which he went so far as to imply that the views of his critics about the efficacy of Soviet countermeasures should not be 'accepted'—by which I sense he means they should be disregarded. Someone not competent to follow the technical nuances of the debate could be forgiven were he to assume that Dr Jastrow's apparent obsession with the long-corrected computational errors reflects a determination to discredit his critics personally.

Dr Ashton Carter, the author of the first report on SDI to be prepared for Congress's Office of Technology Assessment (OTA), is also the target of Dr Jastrow's criticisms. He too has pointed out[21] that Dr Jastrow has never provided his own analysis of the problem. It would be unfortunate if the analysis included such meaningless statements as Jastrow's observation, on page 95 of his book, that one molecule of oxygen always consists of two oxygen molecules bound together. In truth, the precision of Dr Jastrow's style, as manifested in his book, compares poorly with the appearance of scientific exactitude of the papers in which he attacks his critics, and in which he quotes extensively from documents provided him by proponents of SDI at Los Alamos and Livermore. While the voice, like that of Jacob, is obviously Dr Jastrow's, his papers often read as though the hands of more than one Esau had helped steer his pen.

Dr Carter's report of April 1984 considered the technical ideas that were discussed by the Fletcher study team as possible ways for attacking enemy ballistic missiles during their brief boost phase. In preparing it, he was helped by every official organization that was concerned, including Los Alamos and Livermore, as well as the CIA. But the conclusions that he drew were his alone, and the main one was that, 'the prospect that emerging "Star Wars" technologies, when further developed, will provide a perfect or near-perfect defensive system . . . is so remote that it should not serve as the basis of public expectation or national policy about ballistic missile defense.'

Not surprisingly, he was immediately set upon by the proponents of SDI in Los Alamos, Livermore, and the Defense Department—not to mention Dr Jastrow.

Dr Carter's study had been commissioned by OTA at the request of the House Armed Services Committee and the Senate Foreign Relations Committee. In view of the debate that his report stimulated, CTA then undertook an even more extensive study under the scrutiny of an advisory panel, which included among its twenty-one members Michael May, associate director-at-large of Livermore; Robert Clem, the director of systems sciences of the Sandia National Laboratories; senior representatives of several of the major defence contractor companies whc are, or who would be, involved in SDI work; General David Jones, the former chairman of the joint Chiefs of Staff; Robert

McNamara, former Defense Secretary; Gerard Smith, the chief negotiator of the 1972 ABM and the SALT treaties; Major General John Toomay, who had served on the Fletcher study team; as well as Richard Garwin, Sidney Drell, and Ashton Carter, three who have criticized SDI on technical grounds. It would be difficult to conceive of a more distinguished or better balanced group. They advised a project staff which, in addition to the writers of the studies they commissioned and an administrative staff, included nine researchers.

So far as I can judge, the new and lengthy OTA report, *Ballistic Missile Defense Technologies*,[22] and the summary report accompanying it, touch on every aspect of SDI that has been publicly debated, and they set out both sides of every point at issue. The authors and the advisory panel acknowledge that the USSR is 'vigorously developing advanced technologies potentially applicable to BMD.' But at the same time, and contrary to the somewhat equivocal views put forward by the proponents of SDI in order to encourage public support, the OTA report does not consider that the Soviet Union has any lead over the US 'in any of the 20 basic technologies that have the greatest potential for significantly improving military capabilities in the next 10 to 20 years'. (These were the technologies which were reported on in 1985 in the annual report to Congress of the Under-Secretary of Defense for Research and Engineering in the Pentagon.[23])

The OTA report reviews the requirements that an effective BMD system would have to meet in the face of the obvious Soviet countermeasures. The reader is also warned that it is essential to consider more than just the feasibility of a host of separate technical ideas. What matters is operational feasibility—could the developed technical components be combined into an 'integrated, reliable system that could operate effectively and maintain that effectiveness over time as new countermeasures appeared'? The report reaches the same general conclusion that Ashton Carter did in his earlier appraisal—'assured survival of the US population appears impossible to achieve if the Soviets are determined to deny it to us'.

Press reports suggest that the Pentagon's reaction to OTA's new assessment has been less hostile than it was to Ashton Carter's, and that the defence authorities agree that during the years that it would take to move to a defensive strategy, new risks of nuclear conflict might well arise. On the other hand, the head SDI office in Washington believes that even a partial defence would increase the USSR's uncertainties were it ever to contemplate a first strike against the US, and would therefore enhance deterrence. [24]

But while administration and congressional leaders, as well as many press commentators, accept the OTA report as a non-partisan review, which is the way it certainly reads, some diehards have condemned it. What I find surprising is that they have now been joined by Dr Frederick Seitz, the chairman of the Pentagon's Defense Science Board. He and Dr Jastrow recently proclaimed at a meeting of the conservative Heritage Foundation that except for Dr Seitz, all the members of the OTA advisory panel as well as its staff, were strongly prejudiced *ab initio* against SDI. Dr Seitz is also disturbed that the advisory panel did not vote on the report.[25] This, one might suppose, would have been a waste of time, since the vote would surely have gone against SDI in view of his assertion that the majority of those on the panel were in the anti-SDI camp.

General Daniel Graham of High Frontier withdrew from OTA's advisory panel because he anticipated that he would not like the conclusions which were being reached by the study team. He, at least, appears to be committed to SDI whatever the scientific judgment about the programme's technical feasibility.[26] It is an entirely different matter when a scholar of Dr Seitz's eminence[27]—he took General Graham's place on the panel—disavows the report for such reasons as he has so far made public. These reasons add up to a blunt denial of what has been said by critics of SDI about the ability of enemy space mines to destroy battle stations, the ability of 'spoof launches' to confuse space sensors, and so on. Surely the issue of the technological feasibility of the SDI concept has become far too important to the world at large for it to be argued about by accusations of prejudice, whatever the quarter from which they come, rather than by cogent analyses.

If one were to imagine that the President's dream will one day be given substance, far-reaching political and strategic issues will have to be debated, and debated internationally, in a world in which the 1972 ABM Treaty would have become a dead letter, and which in the meantime would undoubtedly have been transformed by major political events. But that could be decades away. Scientific judgments must come first, and they are an entirely different matter. Regardless of whatever political views he may now entertain (he is on record as having declared that the US should be able to make a first strike against the USSR), Dr Seitz should be expected to argue his case before those of his scientific peers who have reached judgments on the facts—some of them in the field of basic science—that are contrary to his.

Dr Jastrow bluntly says that the views of 'professionals', who work full time in the 'defense science community', should be given greater weight than those of their scientific critics, however distinguished they may be, and whatever their previous experience of defence science. Lowell Wood is, not surprisingly, in full agreement. He tells us that Hans Bethe, Richard Garwin, and others who have dared criticize SDI 'have fared uniformly poorly in technical debate in the classified surroundings required by government regulations', and that it is because of their failures in secret conclave that they carry the debate to the public 'immune from the criticism of their technical peers'.[28]

This contemptuous dismissal by Lowell Wood of his critics harmonizes well with his claim that all the technological criticisms of SDI emanate from a few physicists who could be numbered on the fingers of a maimed hand. In any circle where the rules of scientific discourse prevail, both remarks would be dismissed with an equal measure of contempt. Unfortunately laymen who write in favour of SDI and who presume to make judgments on scientific matters about which they have little or no understanding tend to cite any scientific claim—for example Lowell Wood's—that reinforces the entrenched views in which they have a vested interest, be it political or financial. It is highly regrettable, therefore, that many of the most influential and ardent proponents of SDI are politicians and officials such as Richard Perle who have so far displayed surprisingly little critical understanding of the difficulties that the R&D programme entails. It is surely absurd that matters which obviously first need to be strictly judged on their scientific and and technological merits, and which are of such profound importance to the future of life on earth, should be pronounced upon by laymen lacking either a scientific background or any experience in the management of major R&D projects—or both. The technical feasibility of a space-based BMD system is not a matter that will be resolved either by a show of hands, or by a slanging match in which the pro-SDI side on occasion goes so far as to suggest that its critics are soft on communism. The laws of physics and judgments about what is technologically feasible are not yardsticks for the measurement of political attitudes, any more than Galileo's discoveries were disposed of by the conventional dogma of the Church.

RESOLVING THE ARGUMENT

The resolution of the technical argument will depend on the clear formulation of a few basic questions and, following that, on those competent to express a view providing the wisest answers that can be put before the

Administration, Congress, and the people of the world. For example, a fundamental premise, given that a space-based ABM system could be devised, is that beam weapons can be aimed from space at a ballistic missile before it ejects its payload of warheads and penetration aids; that is to say, they can be aimed at a single target and not have to contend with tens and tens of separate targets. If, as Dr Garwin and others have argued, and as the Russians claim, the separation of warheads from the missile can be made to occur within, say, the first hundred kilometres of the atmosphere, then X-ray lasers and particle beams fired from satellites would be relatively useless since they lose their effectiveness when they enter the upper layers of the atmosphere.

The primary question, therefore, is whether a ballistic rocket can be fuelled and programmed to eject its warheads before reaching that height. The recent OTA report, as well as that of Ashton Carter, gave a positive answer to this question, which was what the Fletcher study team also implied the Russians could do, given time. If this is the consensus of those best able to judge, and if the USSR were to seek to achieve the necessary countermeasures over the next decade (if indeed it has not already done so),[29] the complexion of the entire problem of a space-defence system changes completely.[30] One critical part of the SDI concept would evaporate overnight.

Take another question—the enormous number of targets which a space-defence system should be able to engage almost simultaneously. A ship-defence system known as Aegis, which was designed to track two hundred incoming cruise missiles, and to engage sixteen of them at the same time, has not yet been shown to be able to manage two or three.[31] Have the contractors and engineers who have been working for years on airborne and ship defensive systems given their views in public about the engagement pattern that is presumed to be possible in the SDI concept—the destruction every second of between ten and twenty ballistic missiles in a salvo of more than a thousand?

Towering above all such technical issues is the question of whether it could ever be possible to design the computer links that would be needed for a BMD system to function as a whole. This matter, too, is discussed in detail in several reviews, with generally pessimistic conclusions. Dr David Parnas, a consultant of the Office of Naval Research, and an experienced professor of computer science, spelled out in detail his reasons for resigning from the official SDI panel that is dealing with the computer problems of a space-based ABM system.[32] They make formidable reading, adding up as they do to the general conclusion that the job of designing the necessary computer network is an impossible one. In the letter of resignation that covered his detailed submissions, Dr Parnas wrote that he was aware that there were software experts who would disagree with him, and for whom

> the project offers a source of funding, funding that will enrich some personally. . . . During the first sittings of our panel I could see the dollar figures dazzling everyone involved. Al-

most everyone that I know within the military industrial complex sees in the SDI a new 'pot of gold' just waiting to be tapped.

Dr Parnas is fully supported in his view by the computer specialists who have recently founded an organization called Computer Professionals for Social Responsibility. British computer experts have also expressed their scepticism about what has been proposed,[33] and even more recently Herbert Lin of MIT has ended a review of the entire problem by stating that 'no software-engineering technology can be anticipated that will support the goal of a comprehensive ballistic missile defense.'[34] All this is in line with the conclusions of the recently published OTA assessment. The fact that Dr Solomon Buchsbaum of the Bell Laboratories and Dr Danny Cohen of the University of Southern California have publicly expressed more optimistic views, even if they do not claim that error-proof or tested software for the SDI concept could be devised, does not dispose of the criticisms. What is more, it is difficult to imagine the political uproar that would result were the public to become aware that in addition to having its destiny entrusted to a computer network, it was one not free from errors in software. I doubt if SDI could ever surmount this obstacle. It would be worse than having nuclear anti-missiles in one's back yard.

The OTA report undoubtedly reinforced the views about the strategic shortcomings of the SDI concept which have been so powerfully expressed by James Schlesinger, Harold Brown, and Robert McNamara, three former Secretaries of Defense; by General Brent Scowcroft, whom the President had earlier put in charge of the preparation of a major report on the strategic forces of the United States; by Gerard Smith; by at least five of the holders of the office of Director of Defense Research and Engineering since it was established in the late fifties, all of whom know from bitter experience, as I do, how easy it is to waste hundreds and thousands of millions of dollars in the pursuit of a technological will-o'-the-wisp; and by a number of other prominent men who have held public office in the field of national security. There may have been some members of Congress who also found it odd when the Canadian government decided that it wanted no part of the SDI programme, even though any hypothetical space-based defensive system for the United States would automatically provide a shield over Canadian territory. In view of all the doubts, it is no wonder that Congress is keeping a wary eye on the SDI funding.

From time to time we read of major changes in the priorities of the R&D programme. There has even been talk of the early deployment of an unspecified first-phase system. On the other hand, it should not be expected that the setback to the programme will put an end to the work being done in Livermore on nuclear-bomb-pumped X-ray lasers, or at Los Alamos on excimer lasers powered by electron beams. As I have said, both laboratories had embarked on their pet laser and particle-beam projects well before the President spoke in March 1983, and they did so without being disturbed by any thought that the 1972 ABM Treaty barred the development of space-based defence systems, or by the fear that long before any such system could even be devised, the testing of its components would almost certainly constitute an abrogation of the treaty.

There is also no reason to suppose that the men who are working on a super-computer and software for a space defence system are likely to bring their work to a halt because authoritative computer specialists have declared that it will never be possible to devise an acceptable network which could transform the separate components of a space-based BMD into a workable BMD system. The theatrical dream that was the background of the President's challenge to the scientists of America should in retrospect be seen as a proclamation to the world that work on particle beams and high-power lasers was already in progress. In no sense did it set that work in motion. It would be equally sensible and prudent to suppose that research and development work on lasers and particle beams that is going on in the USSR was not halted by the announcement of the American SDI programme.

INTERNATIONAL CONCERN AND THE ABM TREATY

One consequence of the criticisms of the SDI programme has been a reduction of the SDI budget. Another is that many of the explanations that are now given by the administration for the need for the programme to continue differ from the President's original vision and from his view that a defence against ballistic missiles constitutes a higher category of morality than the maintenance of security though the threat of mutual annihilation. One major justification continues to be heard: that the Russians are engaged on work that corresponds to different elements of the SDI programme, and that in many ways they are ahead of the United States. We have also been told that some Russian actions have already breached the terms of the 1972 ABM Treaty. Specific violations are spelled out in impressive brochures. [35]

The Russians counter by pointing to American actions which in their view are breaches of the treaty. They have even offered to suspend work on the much spoken of, and highly vulnerable, vast phased-array radar system which they are building at Krasnoyarsk if the United States abandons its programme to modernize the radar complexes which it has at Fylingdales in the United Kingdom and Thule in Greenland. Their spokesmen argue that these modernization plans, and particularly the rebuilding of Fylingdales as what is rumoured to be a 360–degree phased-array radar complex, is far more questionable than what the USSR is doing at Krasnoyarsk.

A further accusation by the administration is that the USSR has committed 'a far greater investment of plant space, capital, and manpower' to advanced BMD technologies than the US has. [36] This extravagant claim is not borne out by a CIA document about Soviet efforts which was presented to the Armed Services Committee of the Senate on 26 June 1985. [37] Indeed, the document expresses doubt about the applicability of even a network of Krasnoyarsk systems—regarded as the most serious breach of the 1972 treaty—for widespread ABM deployment. Dr Garwin, in a follow-up to testimony presented to a congressional study group on 10 October 1985, has also pointed out that the better part of the large Soviet programme on strategic defence is devoted to the upgrading of its anti-aircraft defence system.[38]

But whatever the truth about Krasnoyarsk, it can hardly be a justification for the US deliberately interpreting the 1972 treaty so widely that the Russians are given cause to say that the US is proposing to contravene the treaty in a much more specific way, or ways, in order to gain the 'advantage' of being able to launch a first strike against the USSR without fear of significant retaliation.

It was therefore unfortunate that immediately before the 1985 Geneva summit, Robert McFarlane, then the head of the National Security Council, declared that no aspect of the development of space-based BMD components is prohibited by the 1972 ABM Treaty, and that what was intended about testing and development merely implied a shift from the technology that was available at the beginning of the 1970s to what can be undertaken today. This statement could be taken as reflecting the hard fact that major vested interests are now involved in the SDI programme—not only the men in the laboratories who started the whole thing and the authorities in the Defense Department who encouraged them, but also the industrialists who see in the SDI programme a bonanza that they cannot afford to disregard. Unfortunately the statement also clearly implied an intended breach of the treaty. Indeed, Gerard Smith has pointed out that what McFarlane implied was not just a breach, but a *new version* of the treaty.[39] That the statement was publicly played down before the President met Mr Gorbachev was therefore only to be expected.

But it remains highly regrettable that the myriad and diverse arguments about SDI have now induced what might well be described as a state of schizophrenia among America's European allies. All of them recognize that the coherence of NATO is a vital consideration, and one that makes it necessary for the United States, as the keystone of the alliance, to be supported in its policies whenever possible. But at the same time there is considerable scepticism in Europe about some of those policies, and particularly about America's nuclear policies, including the SDI programme, which is widely regarded as a threat to the 1972 ABM Treaty and as a spur to the nuclear arms-race. The arguments about the deployment of cruise and Pershing II missiles on European territory caused considerable political trauma and their echoes have not yet faded.[40] It would therefore be a major error of political judgment to treat lightly the fact that vast numbers of Europeans are fearful of any moves that might lead to a further build-up of nuclear armaments, or to assume that any deterioration in the relations between the US and the USSR as a result of SDI would not produce a new wave of anti-nuclear, and indeed of anti-American, protest in Europe.

The agonizing that is now going on about the US invitation to engage in SDI work is already a practical sign of the disquiet and suspicion which are entertained about the President's initiative. Some NATO governments have declined because they dislike the entire idea on political and strategic grounds. The British government agreed to participate in the knowledge that if it refused to provide a formal blessing, SDI scouts were already in the field seeking to entice European specialists with particular skills to work in the United States. Since the 1972 ABM Treaty bars the United States from sharing with others any technology that relates to strategic ballistic missile defence systems, cooperation will do little to help either the economies or the military defences of European countries that formally bless collaboration on R&D, except in so far as such SDI R&D contracts as may be won in probably costly competition with American companies could provide employment for some European scientists and engineers in what may well turn out to be no more than a sharecropping exercise.

Europeans who concern themselves with these matters appreciate that even if the nuclear arsenals of both sides were cut by 50 percent—as has been proposed by both the US and the USSR—more than enough destructive power would still remain, whatever way the cuts were made, to devastate not only the European mainland but also the United States and the western USSR. The concept of nuclear superiority has become meaningless. It belongs to the unreal world of 'nuclear accountancy'. And Europeans no more believe that their countries could be defended by a space-based BMD than they imagine that the USSR would ever risk a first strike either in Europe or against the US. Many suspect that the picture of a layered space-defence system was fabricated in order to confuse the innocent into supposing that a space-based BMD would operate in a measured sequence, a proportion of the offending missiles or warheads being destroyed as they traversed the layers in turn. The greater the number of layers postulated, the more missiles would be destroyed, until in theory—and on paper—almost all were eliminated. But, as I have said, it is the first layer defence that is both decisive and regarded as unfeasible by independent scientists. There are also many European officials who, being concerned with real military security, wonder what SDI has to do with Europe. They know that while it is just conceivable that the Russians might one day attack across the Iron Curtain, their purpose would be to occupy territory—not radioactive territory that had been devastated by nuclear weapons.

The President and Mr Gorbachev now seem to be locked into their respective positions. Time and time again the Russians have declared that if the US continues in its search for a space-based defence system, it will embark upon its own countermeasures, including the further build-up of its offensive forces. This is surely not propaganda. In the Weinberger letter to the President that was leaked just before the Geneva summit, the Defense Secretary warned that 'even a *probable* territorial defense [by the USSR] would require us to increase the number of our offensive forces and their ability to penetrate Soviet defenses to assure that our operational plans could be executed.'[41] That is precisely

what the Russians also say they will do if the US continues to seek, through SDI, to develop a 'territorial
defence'. And, as Mr Nixon has warned,[42] it would be
easy for the Russians to triple in little time the number
of warheads that are carried on their giant SS18s, a
simple multiplication which in theory would by itself
increase the threat that US missile silos face from an
SS18 first strike from three thousand to nine thousand
MIRVed warheads.

Richard Nixon and Henry Kissinger gave their support to SDI because they saw in it both a means whereby
the Russians could be induced to return to Geneva,
and a 'bargaining chip' in arms control negotiations.
But if one were to regard SDI as a bargaining chip, one
would also have to accept that the US will gain only
if it throws it away. If the SDI R&D programme continues, the Russians will respond. Even were SDI to
confound its critics and succeed in the sense that its
separate components could be fitted together in a working system, the United States and the West as a whole
would still lose, not only because the USSR would have
devised measures for defeating a space-based BMD, but
because there are ways other than land-based ICBMs,
for example long range low flying cruise missiles, whereby
the US could be threatened with nuclear devastation.

President Reagan still speaks as though nothing
has changed his original dream. But it has been changed.
He himself changed it when he declared after the Geneva summit that what the United States was embarking
upon was a *non-nuclear* space defensive system. That
declaration, if acted upon, would be the death knell

of the nuclear-pumped X-ray laser, the kernel of the scenario of a defensive astrodome first painted for him by Edward Teller.

Paul Robinson, the principal Associate Director for National Security Programs at Los Alamos, has been quoted as saying that the X-ray laser is in any event flawed because 'it might inadvertently wreak havoc on other SDI components in space,' while his colleague, Steven Rockwood, the Los Alamos Director of SDI Research, asks whether an orbiting device containing a powerful nuclear bomb could ever be politically acceptable.

But, one now has to ask, did an effective X-ray laser ever exist, or could it be made to exist? Whatever the President's motives in insisting that his SDI proposal implied a non-nuclear BMD, his protestations, no doubt inadvertently, coincided with a growing volume of informed comment, based on recently published statements by Livermore itself, to the effect that the claim that an effective nuclear-bomb X-ray laser has been devised was not only premature, but also based upon an unwarranted reading of measurements made in critical tests.[43]

What is more, some directors of SDI research at Livermore have publicly expressed concern because the success of the research for which they are responsible has been exaggerated by Pentagon officials. Dr George Miller, Head of Defense Programs at the Livermore laboratory, has been reported as saying that the public 'is losing sight of how difficult this job is,' while his colleague Dr Cornelius F. Coll III, who is director of

'Star Wars' systems studies at Livermore, declared that 'overstatements by Pentagon officials were imperiling the program. . . . This job is difficult enough without having to defend hyperbole and exaggeration.' It is even reported that a recent demonstration which was laid on to impress a selected audience about the effectiveness of the electromagnetic rail-gun was a spoof. The demonstration pretended to show that a mock-up of a Soviet SS18 missile could be destroyed by the rail-gun. In fact, General Abrahamson is reported by *The New York Times* as having later revealed 'that the damage had not actually been done by an electromagnetic railgun but by a hardened projectile fired from an airgun'—a weapon whose antiquity goes back to the early eighteenth century![44]

Surely the President must now appreciate, possibly even from what Gorbachev told him, what the arguments against SDI are? Surely he realizes that the nuclear arms-race is different in kind from the competition which takes place in the field of conventional arms; that the idea that the US, and USSR, and Europe could ever be subjected to a nuclear conflict is total madness; and that such a conflict could solve nothing? In the forty years since Hiroshima and Nagasaki, increasing numbers of nuclear warheads and delivery systems, not to mention presumed defensive measures, have not provided greater security to any party—not to the United States, not to the USSR, and not to Europe. What they have done is reduce security for all.

We often hear the homely term 'leaky' in the course of the SDI debate, as though if a perfect BMD defence proves impossible, a 'leaky' one would still be worth having. It is yet another of those words which helps to lull the senses so that we fail to realize the hideous reality—that the fraction of warheads that would 'leak' through would today be enough to cause what once used to be euphemistically called 'unacceptable damage'. We continue to talk about numbers of warheads and megatons as though they were numbers of tanks and bomber aircraft. The brutal fact which our minds seem incapable of taking in is that were an explosion to occur over New York or Washington, London or Moscow, one megaton would be equivalent to a million instantaneous deaths (what matter if the figure were 100,000 or 200,000 more or less?).

The President may protest that his SDI dream implies a protection of people and not of silos. But however many times he does so, the fact is that were the 'unthinkable' ever to occur, a future American president would probably never know how his enemy had behaved. He could well have disappeared in the nuclear Armageddon. If the SDI programme ends up only in protecting America's land-based missiles, no president could be sure that given a nuclear outbreak, the Russians would necessarily confine their fire to the American missile fields and not also aim at centres of population, any more than the Russians can be relied upon to believe that the United States would spare their cities. A 'point defence' or SDI II, as some now call it, would, in short, take us back to square one—to the same argument that revealed the futility of missile defences and which ended in the 1972 ABM Treaty.

Adhering to the strictest interpretation of that treaty

has therefore become a vital consideration for all of us—not some so-called liberal interpretation of the way its terms were drafted, however legally argued, not some new version, as Gerard Smith has put it, but the treaty in the sense in which it was negotiated by the two sides. Were some demonstration test of a novel BMD component by either side to result in a unilateral breach, it would be but a short step to the abrogation of the few other treaties that have been so painfully negotiated in order to try to stem the spread of nuclear weapons.

A conflict in which nuclear weapons were used would not help solve any of the political disputes that now divide the two superpowers. It would certainly make it impossible for either to help solve the multitude of territorial and racial disputes and problems of social and economic development which now torment the nations of the world, and in the resolution of many of which both have a common interest. Both leaders should therefore remind themselves of the critical difference between the BMD of the sixties and what is being discussed now. Twenty years ago, active defences against missile attack were being devised by both sides in response to a formulated operational requirement which it was incorrectly assumed could be technically satisfied. Today SDI is a concept that is 'technology led' by the belief that new technological wonders can be fitted together in order to create an effective operational defence system. No one believes that this could happen before the turn of the century, if indeed it ever proves possible. The President knows that in the interval there could well be military conflict.

The two leaders should therefore keep on reminding each other that were the prevailing state of nuclear deterrence to break down, the result could be a catastrophe unparalleled in the history of warfare, and one which would make even the worst natural disaster of which history tells us seem like a gust of wind. The day must surely come when the superpowers, recognizing that both face the same danger of total destruction, stop fencing with nuclear words, and agree to the cut-backs in nuclear arms which both have told the world they are ready to make.

REFERENCES

1. *Essays on Strategy and Diplomacy: The Strategic Defense Initiative*, No. 3, The Keck Center for International Strategic Studies (May 1985).

2. 'If a person leaves his country, leaves his continent, leaves his relatives, leaves his friends, the only people he knows are his professional colleagues. If more than ninety percent of these then come around to consider him an enemy, an outcast, it is bound to have an effect.' Teller, quoted in Blumberg, S. A. and G. Owens, 1976, *Energy and Conflict: The Life and Times of Edward Teller*, New York: Putnam.

3. Blumberg and Owens, p. 411.

4. Broad, William J., 1985, *Star Warriors*, New York: Simon and Schuster.

5. *Science at the Crossroads* (papers from the International Congress of the History of Science and Technology, 1931), 1971, London: Frank Cass.

6. Discovered independently by Charles Townes, an American, and two Russians, N. G. Basov and A. M. Prokhorov, who in 1964 shared a Nobel Prize for their achievement.

7. Carter, Ashton B., April 1984, *Directed Energy Missile*

Defense in Space, Washington, D.C.: US Congress, Office of Technology Assessment.

8. Bethe, Hans A., Jeffrey Boutwell, and Richard L. Garwin, Spring 1985, 'BMD Technologies and Concepts in the 1980s', *Daedelus*, pp. 53–71.

9. Marshall, E., 1985, *Science*, 230, pp. 1249–1251.

10. Jastrow, Robert, 1985, *How to Make Nuclear Weapons Obsolete*, Boston: Little, Brown.

11. Nixon, Richard, 1985, 'Superpower Summitry', *Foreign Affairs*, 64(1).

12. See, for example, Keyworth, George A., 1985, *Security and Stability* (IGOC Policy Papers No. 1), University of California, San Diego.

13. In Congressional testimony (22 April 1985) Dr Jastrow admitted that he had not carried out any analysis of SDI on his own, and that he had made it his business to translate into lay language the views of government scientists.

14. Elsewhere in the book he claims that it would take only five years, which I presume means by 1990.

15. Union of Concerned Scientists, March 1984, *Space Based Missile Defense*.

16. Union of Concerned Scientists, 1984, *The Fallacy of Star Wars*, New York: Vintage Books.

17. See Richard L. Garwin's testimony to the Senate Armed Services Committee (24 April 1984) and his 'How many orbiting lasers for boost-phase intercept', 1985, *Nature*, 815, pp. 286–290.

18. Garwin, Richard L., and Edward T. Gerry, 'Fifteen Agreed Propositions on SDI', publicly presented at Dartmouth College, 23 May 1985.

19. US Department of Defense, *The Strategic Defense Initiative Defensive Technologies Study*, Washington D.C., March 1984.

20. Jastrow, Robert, 1985, *Journal of International Affairs*, 39(1), pp. 45–55.

21. *Commentary*, March 1985.

22. US Congress, Office of Technology Assessment, 1985, *Ballistic Missile Defense Technologies*.

23. US Congress, 1985, *The Fiscal Year 1986 Department of Defense Program for Research, Development and Acquisition*.

24. *International Herald Tribune*, 27 September 1985.

25. *Nature*, 1985, **318**, 3.

26. Beardsley, T., 1985, *Nature*, **314**, 7.

27. Dr Seitz is a former President of the National Academy of Sciences and of Rockefeller University. He also served a term as chairman of the NATO Science Committee.

28. *Commentary*, March 1985. Not surprisingly, Wood's assertion has been denied by Garwin and others who have participated in secret debates with Livermore scientists. It is interesting too that at a Congressional hearing in 1985 Teller cited Hans Bethe's opinion in support of an optimistic statement he was making about the X-ray lasers. He said that having discussed the matter with Livermore scientists, Bethe now agreed with him, which Bethe subsequently denied. Ironically, one of Teller's well-known public themes—ploy might be a better word—is to decry the evils of secrecy, beyond the veils of which he is not unknown to vanish when challenged.

29. See *Space-Strike Arms and International Security*, Report of the Committee of Soviet Scientists for Peace Against the Nuclear Threat, Moscow, October 1985.

30. Ashton Carter's views were strongly supported by Major General John C. Toomay, a member of Dr Fletcher's study team, in his rejoinder (22 June 1984) to the Department of Defense's criticisms of the Carter report.

31. 'Star Wars: SDI, The Grand Experiment,' *Spectrum* (American Institute of Electrical and Electronic Engineers), September 1985.

32. Parnas, David L., 1985, 'Software Aspects of Strategic Defense Systems,' *American Scientist*, 73, pp. 432–440.

33. *New Scientist*, 31 October 1985.

34. 'The Development of Software for Ballistic Missile Defense', *Scientific American*, December 1985, pp. 32–39.

35. *Soviet Directed Energy Weapons Perspectives on Strategic Defenses*, CIA, March 1985; *Soviet Acquisition of Militarily Significant Western Technology: An Update*, September 1985; *Soviet Strategy Defense Programs*, Department of Defense and Department of State, October 1985; Richard Perle, 'The Soviet Record on Arms Control', *The National Interest*, Fall 1985.

36. *Soviet Strategic Defense Programs*, Department of Defense and Department of State, October 1985, p. 12.

37. Gates, Robert M., and Lawrence K. Gershwin, 1985, 'Soviet Strategic Force Developments'. Testimony to the Senate Armed Services Committee, 26 June.

38. In a submission to Congressman Mrazek (10 October 1985), in which he also pointed out that the Stanford University Workshop on Strategic Missile Defense, of which he was a member, recommended (April 1985) that the United States should fund an adequate programme of work on offensive countermeasures to Soviet SDI, including work on powerful lasers.

39. *The New York Times*, 23 October 1985.

40. For example, on 3 December 1985, the Netherlands government declared that having finally agreed to the stationing of the complement of cruise missiles assigned to it, as compensation it was going to abandon two other nuclear roles which had for long been its responsibility in the NATO strategic plan.

41. *Boston Sunday Globe*, 24 November 1985.

42. See note 11.

43. For the above statements by Robinson, Rockwood, and Livermore, see Smith, R. Jeffrey, *Science*, **230** (8 November 1985), pp. 646–648 and (29 November 1985), p. 1023; *Los Angeles Times* (12 November 1985).

44. For the statements by Miller, Coll, and Abrahamson, see Broad, William J., *The New York Times*, 16 December 1985.

PART
TWO

5

The Prospects of Nuclear War

Hawks, Doves, and Owls[1] is the report of the 'Avoiding Nuclear War' project carried out at the John F. Kennedy School of Government at Harvard. Some of its contributors have had direct experience of policy-making circles in Washington. In addition, its editors, Graham Allison, Albert Carnesale, and Joseph Nye, Jr, all of Harvard, have a clear message. The protection of US values and institutions is absolutely dependent on the avoidance of nuclear war. And since no one can know how such a war might be set off or, if started, controlled, that imperative need is also dependent on the avoidance of any war in which the Western Alliance and Warsaw Pact powers might become embroiled. What is more, the three editors recognize that 'the nuclear threat creates a solidarity of interest between the two superpowers—against a total war in which they would be the greatest victims.'

It is against this background, and on the sensible assumption that 'US-Soviet rivalry, superpower interest in Europe, and Third World instability' are unlikely to change in the near future, that the six scholars who contribute the specialized essays in this book consider how things could go wrong. The editors provide the introductory chapter, which sets out what they call the 'agenda', and they end the book with recommendations for action.

The first chapter, on accidental nuclear war, is by Paul Bracken of Yale. Whatever might have been the situation in years gone by, he argues, technological and organizational developments have made it all but inconceivable that a war could erupt today as a result of the sort of accident that is often discussed—for example because a nuclear weapon had been launched after an operator had incorrectly interpreted radar blips made by a flock of geese, or because of a failed computer chip, or even through the action of a 'crazed military officer'. There are many who are not as optimistic, among them Daniel Ford, who has also made a study of the subject.

Bracken is more worried about trouble arising from maritime accidents in which ships or submarines are sunk and where the conclusion might be drawn that they had been attacked as part of a larger plan. He has pointed out 'that the danger of accidental and inadvertent war' would be 'considerable during a crisis involving the United States and the Soviet Union. . . . Unfortunately', as he has written, 'our conception of the dangers of inadvertent war are formed in peacetime, creating an unjustified complacency about the ability of government to control events during a crisis.'[2] What is needed is a continuous channel of communication between the American and Russian authorities. For the rest, he wants the US to concentrate its 'energy on preventing confrontations', and the establishment of 'design principles and rules of the road' to deal with periods of intense crisis. He is also worried because he has a hunch that Britain, France, and China 'have given even less thought to these issues than the United States has.' If what he writes is an indication of how far the US has got in formulating 'rules of the road' to deal with the danger of unintentional nuclear war, the three countries he mentions will not however have far to go before they find themselves up against a brick wall.

In the essay that follows, Richard Betts, formerly a staff member of the Senate Select Committee on Intelligence, and now of the Brookings Institution, deals with surprise attack and pre-emption. From him we learn that the Russians keep their forces 'on lower levels of day-to-day alert' than does the US. This is also stated in a later chapter by Stephen Meyer, who deals specifically with 'Soviet Perspectives on the Paths to Nuclear War'. Betts rates very low the possibility that either side would embark upon a preventive war, since in a nuclear age such a step might well be suicidal. The only circumstance in which he can conceive of the US risking a pre-emptive attack would be when a state of tension had come about because political changes in the world order were moving decisively in the Russian favour, and when the US had a chance of limiting the scale of nuclear retaliation by means of a first strike at the Russian missile silos.

Here, however, is the problem. It is inconceivable

that the US would launch a pre-emptive surprise attack unless it was certain that nuclear war was inevitable. But who would say that it was? 'A cool and rational decision to this effect by a collective body is hard to imagine.' Both sides deploy a 'triad' of nuclear forces, including missiles based on land, in the air, and at sea. Since this in effect means that both possess an invulnerable second-strike force, the price of a pre-emptive strike would be the high risk of national suicide—regardless of who had attacked first. In order 'to ensure consistency between political aims and military signals,' both sides, Betts argues, therefore clearly need to be 'thoroughly educated in the dynamics of military alerts and crisis deployments'. And in this respect, he implies, there is greater coherence today on the Soviet than on the American side.

In effect this theme is taken up by Fen Hampson, who deals with the problem of maintaining peace in Western Europe. A possible 'scenario' of how this could be broken is outlined by the editors in their introduction. An uprising might take place in East Germany which the authorities could not suppress; Russian troops would be called in to help; West Germans would infiltrate to help their brothers in the East; the Russians would block all the roads to West Berlin; a NATO supply airlift would be resisted by the Russians; and so on until there is full-scale land war with the risk of nuclear escalation.

Hampson considers other possibilities—for example, that there might be 'a general loosening of the Western alliance that created opportunities for Soviet adventurism, or a deterioration in Eastern Europe that tempted the United States to reverse the Yalta accords, or, more likely, some combination of the two.' War could spread to Europe from the Middle East. There might also be changes in the balance of forces, particularly in the credibility of the US commitment to launch its strategic nuclear forces in the presumed defence of Europe.

When he considers the balance of forces, Hampson sensibly associates himself with those who, now that both sides have a superfluity of warheads, are not impressed by what he calls 'bean counts' and what others refer to as 'nuclear accountancy'. He is also concerned about the instability that would result from futile efforts to devise defences against ballistic missiles. But the most important and immediate danger is that a major disruption of the political *status quo* could lead to hostilities between the NATO and Warsaw Pact powers, hostilities which, once started, could move on to nuclear disaster. If we are to continue to avoid war in Europe, there should never be any ambiguity about NATO's intentions of a kind that could invite a pre-emptive attack by Warsaw Pact forces. For example, tactical nuclear weapons should not be deployed in a way that invites pre-emption or accidental launch. NATO's conventional forces should always be adequate to deal with those they face. Equally important is a sensible political strategy to govern NATO in its dealings with the Warsaw Pact powers.

It is interesting that the Stockholm International Peace Research Institute has also put out a book arguing along the same lines as does Fen Hampson.[3] It is also worth noting that a recent study by Daniel Frei, carried out in cooperation with the United Nations Institute for Disarmament Research,[4] agrees that the chances of an unauthorized nuclear war are 'practically zero' but warns that one could start unintentionally, not only as escalation from a conventional war but because of a multitude of causes, all compounded in different degrees of 'misjudgment, miscalculation or misunderstanding'.

Francis Fukuyama's chapter, 'Escalation in the Middle East and Persian Gulf', parallels Hampson's on Europe in so far as it provides a balanced account of the dangerous turns that events could take in the vast and troubled region stretching from Morocco in the west to Pakistan in the east. Ever since the end of World War II and the breakup of the old British and French colonial and imperial orders, and ever since the foundation of the state of Israel, there has rarely, if ever, been a moment when two or more of the countries concerned were not at one another's throats. The stranglehold on Western economies of the Middle East OPEC countries has also become a major disruptive issue, in which the interests of the US and the Soviet Union conflict. Both, however, have an obvious interest in avoiding hostilities, and Mr Fukuyama rightly insists that the 'single most important factor' influencing the outcome of past crises has been 'political prudence on the part of national leaders'—hence the importance of cultivating 'friendly talk' and better communications between the US and the USSR.

The likelihood of the superpowers being drawn into a catalytic nuclear war through their opposing interests in some dispute involving a third country, or because of the nefarious activities of some terrorist organization, is not rated highly by Henry Rowen in his contribution to *Hawks, Doves, and Owls*. He too sees a clear community of interest between the two superpowers. But as Stephen Meyer, a consultant to the CIA and the Defense Department, remarks in another essay, it is not always easy to understand the official Soviet views about nuclear matters. As he puts it, we have no Russian memoirs on the subject, no transcripts of public governmental hearings, no talkative officials who have moved out of Moscow, as they do out of Washington, into industry or a university.

Meyer, a professional student of Soviet affairs, has little faith in publicly proclaimed Soviet military doctrine and policy, or in pronouncements clearly made for propaganda purposes. He does not mention it, but the way Khrushchev made it his business at the beginning of the sixties to mislead the US about the missile strength of the USSR is a case in point. In order to discern what can be learned about 'Soviet perspectives on the paths to nuclear war', he prefers to extract what meaning he can from such published material as is available about Russian military plans, force structure and deployment, and from an analysis of Soviet diplomatic behaviour. He reminds his readers that 'throughout the 1950s Soviet leaders watched as tens, then hundreds, of American "strategic" delivery systems were deployed around the Soviet periphery,' with the not surprising consequence that the Russians are convinced that the US is committed to their destruction. Whichever way hostilities could begin, the Russians still fear a nuclear bolt from the blue.

Meyer also reminds us that, despite this fear, Soviet nuclear forces are always at a lower state of alert than are the American, and that Soviet nuclear weapons are not entrusted to the military as a whole, but are in the charge of an elite and specialist body which he believes has some connection with the KGB. Today only Russian ICBMs are on day-to-day alert and loaded with nuclear warheads, ready to retaliate against a US first strike. 'No Soviet strategic bombers are on alert,' while 'only a comparatively small fraction of Soviet SLBMs are available at any given time for second-strike retaliation under surprise attack conditions.' 'Despite popular impressions,' Mr Meyer continues—and one has to suppose that as a CIA and Defense Department consultant he should know—'most of the Soviet military machine is not geared up to go to war at a moment's notice.' Hence Soviet military doctrine implies 'other possible paths to nuclear war'.

His view is that the Russian leaders now believe that nuclear hostilities could not occur except as a result of some major crisis and confrontation or as an escalation of conventional wars. Any form of 'NATO nuclear use' would 'unleash a massive and devastating Soviet theater nuclear strike against all NATO military facilities.' This would escalate to global nuclear war only if the Soviet homeland were hit by American weapons, say Pershing IIs or cruise missiles based on the Western European mainland. Even then, the Politburo, not the military, would be the ones who would authorise a retaliatory strike. In an article in *Foreign Affairs*, Albert Wohlstetter also argues forcefully that the Politburo keeps 'the use of nuclear weapons under continuing control.'[5] What matters therefore is the close political understanding that exists between the Politburo and the high military command. Be this as it may, Dr Meyer warns that no Westerner could ever predict how the Soviets would react to a nuclear strike, from wherever it came. I suppose the Russians are equally in the dark about how the West would respond to an attack they might launch.

Although *Hawks, Doves, and Owls* is based on long and lengthy collaboration, the two essays in which the editors sum up its findings are a bit of a letdown. The preface tells us that the book is addressed first to 'members of the policymaking community', next to interested citizens, and third to 'experts on nuclear weapons and international security'. The stylized presentation of a list of 'dos and don'ts' about how to avoid nuclear war might well help the interested reader to organise his thoughts on the subject. But I am doubtful whether such a list, plus a few simple tables and diagrams, could ever be taken seriously either by political leaders or by their military advisers.

For example, do they need to be warned that it is wise to maintain a credible nuclear deterrent given that one is deployed by their potential enemy; or that cities cannot by defended against nuclear attack; or that conventional forces should be strengthened; or that the

Soviet Union should not be provoked; or that the West, i.e., the US, should plan for ending a war if one begins; or that the US should 'expect the unexpected'; or that nuclear weapons should not be treated as other weapons? These homilies are merely statements of the obvious, and they hardly do justice to the other essays in *Hawks, Doves, and Owls*. It would have been a different matter if the book had specifically explained when a nuclear force becomes 'incredible', or when 'enough is enough' or what degree of so-called modernization can be undertaken without destabilizing the present state of mutual deterrence. But such matters are left untouched.

Perhaps the project was launched with altogether too ambitious an aim. How could there be a textbook that described what should or should not be done, given this or that political crisis, as a physician might resort to a computerized data bank of the signs and symptoms of disease? It is inconceivable that any such book would have been consulted in the Cuban crisis of 1962, or would be were such a crisis to recur. The story of how President Kennedy and his close advisers conducted themselves during that period of confrontation is well known and was in fact the subject of a book by Graham Allison, one of the editors of *Hawks, Doves, and Owls*. I do not know what ordinary people in the United States believed was going to happen, but in Europe fear of a nuclear war was widespread. Moreover, no one knew what to do about it.

The British were kept closely informed about the progress of events, particularly as the UK ambassador to Washington, the late Lord Harlech (David Ormsby-Gore at the time), was a close friend of the President. On the assumption that the 'nuclear balloon' was bound to go up when the President's ultimatum expired, the top officials of the British defence establishment were summoned to a meeting at 9 am on Sunday, 28 October. Just as they sat down, the news came on the radio that Khrushchev had agreed to President Kennedy's demands, including the removal of the missiles and the dismantling of the missile sites.

We looked at one another in relief. Had hostilities broken out in the Caribbean, there was a possibility that the Russians would have immediately imposed a new blockade of Berlin, or taken some other action that would have brought war to Europe. But we had no contingency plans. I remember Lord Mountbatten, chairman of the British Chiefs then saying, 'What would we have done if the Russians had not backed down? We must work this out.' There was no answer. I am sure that were a similar situation to arise tomorrow, it too would not be dealt with, whether in Washington, Moscow, or Brussels, according to a synthesis and analysis of past decisions and past judgments. Military crises do not spring full-blown on to the centre of the stage in accordance with a given pattern. Suez, Cuba, Korea, Vietnam, the Falklands, Lebanon—each was different, each built up differently, and each could have evolved and ended differently from the way it did.

Even if one were to assume that guidelines and rules of conduct of the kind spelled out in the final chapter of *Hawks, Doves, and Owls* could have prac-

tical value, a necessary condition would be that Paul
Bracken is right when he assures us that we need not
worry about malfunctions of a mechanical kind in the
nuclear system, or about some sergeant or major starting a nuclear war in a fit of madness. For if the system
could, as it were, operate on its own—or fail to operate
when it was commanded to do so—there would be an
even more unpredictable set of circumstances to worry
about in addition to the political and other possible
upsets the book lays before us. And to Daniel Ford,
the control of the nuclear system is nothing near as
reliable as Bracken would have us believe.

A *New Yorker* journalist, Mr Ford sets out his
reasons for this view in *The Button*,[6] which is based on
a lengthy series of interviews, mostly with unnamed
people who presumably were military personnel and
should not have told him all they did. We learn that
the Defense Department and the Joint Chiefs are largely
dependent on commercial communications networks
in maintaining their worldwide military command and
control. Relay stations are in vulnerable places, and
some critical parts of the early warning system against
a missile attack have been 'off the air' for some time
because they are waiting for new computers or for
thermionic valves to be replaced by modern solid-
state devices.

A computer at NORAD, the nerve centre of the
US defence system in Cheyenne Mountain near Col-
orado Springs, does not work. The one-star general who
was showing Mr Ford around explained what each of
five telephones on the NORAD commander's battle-

station desk was for, but when the obliging officer picked up the telephone connecting directly with the White House, there was no one at the other end. Dr John Steinbruner of the Brookings Institution, and once a member of the official world of Washington, told Mr Ford that 'given the extreme vulnerability of the entire [command and control] mechanism to the pre-emptive moves of the opponent', the American strategic nuclear force was 'primed to go—massively'.

This and other bits of information lead Mr Ford to conclude that a command system which is 'unready to deliver orders for retaliation but streamlined to convey commands for a first strike unmistakably suggests the basic intent of its designers.' So far as he is concerned, 'the stated [US] national policy of retaliation' is merely 'official rhetoric'. If the President had to decide without delay whether to launch or not to launch a nuclear strike against the USSR, he could not rely on getting together with his closest advisers, the Secretaries of State and Defense. Mr Ford's authority for telling us this is Henry Kissinger, whom he quotes as saying that the only way US strategy could be implemented would be by delegating authority to some field commander 'who must be given discretion so that when he thinks a nuclear war has started, he can retaliate.'

If this is indeed the situation, if even half of what Daniel Ford tells us about the inadequacies of the US command and control system is true, the Avoiding Nuclear War project of the Kennedy School either overlooked some central questions or did not treat them in sufficient depth.

First, can a 100-percent trust ever be placed in any command and control system on which the fate of a nation could rest, and particularly on one which depends overwhelmingly upon electrical and electronic relays? It takes time—decades—to construct even the kind of early warning system against a missile attack that we believe we have now. During that time technology changes, so that elements which were introduced when the system was designed need to be updated and replaced as later components are added. Ford tells us that the information from current US warning systems is transmitted to 1960s computers, which were built to analyse a strike of some fifty warheads. If they had to deal with a strike involving thousands of missiles or decoys, they would be overwhelmed with data and could assess neither the size of the attack nor the likely targets. Much the same could be said of our anti-aircraft defences. Were that not the case, why should there now be mention, in discussions of President Reagan's Strategic Defense Initiative, of the need to update the anti-aircraft defence systems that started to be built in the fifties?

Those who have the responsibility of translating into hardware the President's concept of a defence in space against ballistic missiles know how formidable are the technological hurdles that need to be overcome. As the President would have learned from an official panel which was set up in 1983 under Mr Fred Hoffman to consider the strategic implications of his proposed SDI, an imperfect defence, one which could only deal with a small but not a full-scale attack, would be a provocative step.[7] Even if a defensive space astrodome were possible, it could not prevent nuclear weapons getting beneath it or past it. And we know that in the world of abstractions with which strategic analysts deal, the idea of controlling escalation, even if one assumed a perfect command and control system, is nonsense unless the two opposing sides were to co-operate closely. In any event, if an early warning system as well as all its related systems did work, and a nuclear launch was signalled, it would be too late. Nuclear war would have begun.

Because of his concern that an all-out nuclear exchange could result not only in mutual suicide, but also in the kind of global catastrophe now called nuclear winter, Wohlstetter, in his *Foreign Affairs* article, sets out a scenario in which the two superpowers come to some kind of agreement restricting the use of nuclear weapons to military targets only, so as to avoid extensive civilian deaths and to keep the conflict limited. This would be fine—so far as it goes, and given that the actual military world resembled the one that armchair strategists invent so easily, and if there were mutual agreement, indeed international agreement, about what constituted military targets.

The reality is that no military leader, no one who has carried the responsibility of command in the European theatre, can genuinely believe that he knows what would happen once one side had fired a nuclear weapon. The initiative would then pass immediately to the opposing side, regardless of what may be written in the tactical handbooks that assume the use of nuclear weapons (both sides have to have such handbooks to accord even abstract meaning or credibility to the deployment of such weapons). Moreover, the belief that nuclear weapons could be used in battle carries with it the implication that the authority vested in the supreme command for their use would have to be quickly delegated to army commanders, corps commanders, and even to divisional commanders. Such authority would have to be delegated right down to the level where the tide of battle had moved in such a way that, at least in theory, what happened next could be influenced by one or more nuclear shots delivered at targets at some distance from one's own troops. Once this happened, there could be no central control. To the best of my knowledge, every nuclear war game that has been played out realistically on the basis of actual military dispositions in the European theatre has shown that the result would be mutual military disaster with, in addition, millions of civilian deaths, even when it was assumed that the nuclear exchange had not become intercontinental. The hard fact is that there is no more reason to suppose that an exchange of nuclear fire could be restrained in a field war than there is to suppose that an inter-continental exchange of destruction could be. One could only hope.

We therefore need to ask whether the civil power could discharge its responsibilities of control in a moment of real nuclear crisis. How would the President know when to delegate the authority that Henry Kissinger is quoted as saying would have to be delegated? Daniel Ford tells us that in addition to the President,

SAC and the National Military Command Center in the Pentagon also hold the 'codes' for a retaliatory response. But these are the military executive agencies whereby a political decision would be implemented— they are not the elected representatives of the people. In the event of the death of the President, how does authority pass, in conformity with the Constitution, to the Vice-President or to the Speaker of the House? How does the high military command and everyone else learn that authority has passed—and to whom?

How, indeed, in the event of a crisis—for example a first strike by the USSR—could the President consult or inform the members of Congress? And given the inadequacies of the communications network, how could the President consult his allies, and they one another? When Prime Minister Attlee flew to see President Truman in November 1950, there was time for him to express Britain's disquiet at the rumour that America might use a nuclear weapon against North Korea in order to prevent the total disintegration of MacArthur's forces. Today there would be no time.

And what about the disciplined dependence of the military on the political authority? It is a fact of history that the high commands exert their own pressures in times of acute political crisis. General MacArthur did not see eye to eye with President Truman, but the President had time to dismiss him. The Pentagon brought considerable pressure to bear upon President Kennedy in the Cuban crisis—but the President's judgment was able to prevail. What is the position today? Daniel Ford quotes a former Pentagon official as saying that while

Sergeant Bilko can't start World War III today, General Bilko certainly can. Can he?

Scott Sagan, who participated in the Avoiding Nuclear War project of the Kennedy School, and who is now a member of a Joint Chiefs of Staff directorate which deals with nuclear and chemical warfare, has thrown some light on this question in an article that was published separately.[8] It deals with three nuclear alerts, those of May 1960, at the time of the first U-2 incident, of October 1962, at the time of the Cuban crisis, and of October 1973, at the time of the Middle East war, and is probably the most detailed and revealing analysis of official and now accessible information about nuclear crises that has ever seen the light of day. He tells us that there are five gradations of nuclear alert, beginning with 'fade-out' and ending with the most acute, 'cocked-pistol'. The three cases of alert that he analyses were initiated at the presidential level. The Joint Chiefs who received the order in turn issued their instructions in a way that permitted a somewhat higher level of alert than the political authority intended. Base commanders then went even higher. The point Sagan is making is that the civil authority does not appreciate sufficiently the 'degree to which alert authority rests in the hands of individual military commanders . . . who can take what they judge are necessary steps to protect their forces.' He also writes that there is no evidence that the Russians responded in 1973 by alerting their nuclear forces, and that their response in 1962, before they backed off in Cuba, was less menacing than the US response.

The McMahon Act of 1946 placed America's nuclear arsenal under civilian control. Today it is under that of the military. This is clearly a dilution of presidential authority, however much the release of nuclear warheads may be held in check by electronic locks and by operational procedures. But again, what degree of authority *is* delegated to the military so that they can deal speedily with urgent crises? Stephen Meyer believes that in the USSR the KGB, which is an executive arm of the Politburo, has a part in controlling the release of Russian nuclear warheads. It would have helped if we knew more about the way this is done.

It would also have helped if we were told something about the exact constitutional authority of the high military command in the US. The military have no authority to start wars. Deciding that events had so developed that military action was called for would be a political judgment, whether the country was the victim of aggression or if the government decided to undertake military action in defence of a critical national interest. In the United Kingdom the Chiefs of Staff would have the responsibility to advise whether defence or attack was likely to succeed, or whether, whatever the circumstances, defeat was a certainty. Today it would be absurd to suppose that any top military adviser would encourage his political masters to go to war when success was clearly impossible or when nuclear annihilation of their country was the likely outcome. If the political authority decided to go ahead despite such advice, its military advisers would have to comply—or resign.

President Truman is said to have had on his desk a notice saying 'The buck stops here.' The buck is now, to some extent, in the hands of the military, and in consequence, if Mr Ford has not been misled, the man who might press the doomsday button could well be a general, even though, were he rational, he would know that he had no more than a marginal chance of keeping a nuclear war under control. He would also certainly know that 'war' could immediately mean the deaths of hundreds of thousands, of perhaps millions, with disintegrating skyscrapers hurtling through others as they collapsed, in cities where the streets had disappeared. It would be a vision of a hundred or even a thousand Hiroshimas. When the fires died down, a radioactive breeze would soothe the dead in the cooling rubble of Washington, New York, Moscow, Leningrad, and Paris, as winter closed in. The word 'war' cannot and should not be used in association with the term 'nuclear'.

What the leaders of both sides therefore need to ask is what imaginable political prize would be worth such a risk. Of course it is conceivable that were the US and the USSR to use nuclear weapons against each other, one side might throw in the sponge after a few days—given that anyone was left in authority to do that—after both had suffered millions of deaths. And then what? I suppose that such a war could start as in the scenario suggested in *Hawks, Doves, and Owls*— with an uprising in East Germany. But who says that in the rumbling phases leading to hostilities NATO would not disintegrate; that France and the United Kingdom would not keep out of the subsequent conflict? In a world of peace, a reunited Germany is an understandable goal, but if a war that might go nuclear were started to bring union about, there would be no Germanies to unite.

President Reagan has said that a nuclear war cannot be won, and must never be fought. So have Russian leaders. Presumably neither the President nor Mr Gorbachev would have reached his present high office if those by whom he was elected or selected had felt that their candidates were so simple as to regard nuclear war, with its inevitable consequences, as a military option to be considered seriously in some circumstances, or if either had declared publicly that in order to achieve some political purpose he might risk a lightning holocaust that could bring death to scores of millions of his fellow citizens. 'Better dead than red,' and its converse, 'Better the grave than capitalism,' might have been meaningful slogans in the days when the US and the USSR possessed only small nuclear arsenals, when the degree of nuclear devastation might have been limited.

Today they have an empty ring. There is no alternative to peace between the superpowers, which is another way of stating the message of *Hawks, Doves, and Owls*. The most urgent issue which the United States and the USSR now face is the avoidance of war with each other. Political differences cannot be allowed to drive them there. Neither should be drawn into a catalytic or accidental nuclear war. Both should be concerned to prevent nuclear proliferation. Both have to avoid any step that could lead to the destabilization of the present state of mutual nuclear deterrence. Above all, neither can afford to commit its future to the operation of automated systems of command and control which might either be technically defective or which, by their very perfection, could foreclose the workings of human judgment.

REFERENCES

1. Allison, G. T., A. Carnesale and J. S. Nye (eds), 1985, *Hawks, Doves and Owls: An Agenda for Avoiding Nuclear War*, New York: Norton.
2. Bracken, Paul, 1985, Letter to *New York Review of Books* (5 December).
3. Nincic, Miroslaw, 1985, *How War Might Spread to Europe*, Stockholm: SIPRI.
4. Frei, Daniel, 1983, *Risks of Unintentional Nuclear War*, London: Croom Helm.
5. Wohlstetter, Albert, 1985, 'Between an unfree world and none: Increasing our choices,' *Foreign Affairs*, 63(5), pp. 962–994.
6. Ford, Daniel, 1985, *The Button: The Pentagon's Strategic Command and Control System*, New York: Simon and Schuster.
7. *Contribution to the Future Strategy Study*, submitted to the Secretary of Defense.
8. Sagan, Scott D., 1985, 'Nuclear alerts and crisis management,' *International Security*, 9(4), pp. 99–139.

6

The Politics of Outer Space

By good fortune—indeed, almost by accident—Professor Walter A. McDougall has provided us with a timely record of the technological and political events that form the background to today's urgent debate about the military exploitation of space.[1] After failing to get the approval of his colleagues at the University of California at Berkeley for a book about World War I, he decided to tackle the political history of the early space age. It illustrated, as he saw it, not only the difficulties encountered in the international management of 'nonterritorial' regions, but also the 'interplay of international rivalry and technological change.'

Professor McDougall starts by detailing the steps that culminated in 1957 in the launch of the first Sputnik. From there the story moves to the present, when more than 5,000 'objects', which include 200 to 300 operating satellites, are being constantly tracked by radar as they orbit the earth in the company of innumerable pieces of man-made space debris. Whatever argument there may be about Professor McDougall's views of the impact of the advance of technology on political and social change, all who are concerned about the critical state of international relations today will be grateful to him for having spared no effort in tracking down any information that could be relevant to the history of space technology—Russian as well as American.

At the start of the story there were no politics. They were not brought into the fictional world of space travel that Jules Verne created, nor had they any role in H. G. Wells's fanciful Martian invasion of 1898. But long before these writers took up their pens, it was known that our globe is a planet that in the course of a year traverses, at a speed of nearly 70,000 miles an hour, an elliptic path of some 580 million miles around the sun, with the moon held within the gravitational field of the earth, around which it revolves at a speed of nearly 2,300 miles an hour. It was also known that other planets in the solar system move in fixed paths in accordance with the gravitational forces that the sun exerts on them, and which to a lesser extent they exert on each other. It was also clear that if it ever became possible to shoot a man from the earth beyond the limits of its atmosphere at a speed sufficient to counteract the gravitational force that would otherwise pull him back, he would float weightless in space around the globe, or he would fly, if he had been propelled with sufficient velocity, to the moon and the stars.

From Professor McDougall we learn that the first person to apply a scientific mind to these possibilities, and particularly to the problem of rocket-powered flight in space, was the Russian Konstantin Tsiolkovsky. By the 1880s, this single-minded genius was writing about the impact that the condition of zero-gravity exercises on the classical laws of motion. He also conceived of reactive flight outside the atmosphere two decades before heavier-than-air flight within it became a reality. He knew how to calculate the velocity—about five miles a second—at which an object of given weight had to be shot into space in order to coast around the globe, and also the escape velocity of some seven miles a second needed to carry it beyond the earth's gravitational field. Correspondingly, Tsiolkovsky knew how to calculate the power or thrust that a rocket would need to generate in order to achieve these required speeds. By 1903 he had published a treatise on 'the mathematics of orbital mechanics and designed a rocket powered by the (precocious) combination of liquid oxygen and liquid hydrogen'.

If the Russians did not succeed in building rockets with the power necessary to take men into space before Hitler's invasion of Poland in 1939, they certainly built smaller ones. For Tsiolkovsky was not the only Russian to be enthused by the prospects of flight both within and beyond the earth's atmosphere, and even about the possibility of establishing human colonies in space. Yuri Kondratyuk, one of his colleagues, early on proposed the use of solar power in spacecraft, and considered the design of landing craft or modules for lunar and planetary visits. 'The Soviet Union,' Professor McDougall tells us, 'was the first government to endorse and support the goal of spaceflight.' An Institute of Aerodynamics already existed (it was founded in 1906), but in 1918, immediately after the Revolution, the new government decided to establish a Central Aerodynamics Institute. A Central Bureau for the Study of the Problems of Rockets followed in 1924.

Enthusiasm for space was not confined to Russia, but other industrialized countries lagged far behind. In the United States the 'jealous and secretive' Robert Goddard worked alone, experimenting with liquid-fuel rockets as far back as 1926. By the time the Second World War started, he had built a rocket 22 feet long, which carried enough fuel to develop an average thrust of 825 pounds. Some members of the Army's ordnance plants were also trying to develop small rockets for air-to-air combat, but Goddard's idiosyncratic isolation meant that neither his vision nor his achievements attracted the effective attention of the authorities, in the way that the work of Tsiolkovsky, Kondratyuk, F. A. Tsander, and many others had done in Russia.

In Germany events moved differently. As early as 1929 the army had called for the development of a liquid-fuel rocket, and a year or so later work was started on the design of a jet-powered engine for aircraft. Wernher von Braun, a highly ambitious and personable young engineer, was recruited, and by the autumn of 1939 he and his team had moved to an isolated test-site at Peenemünde. What happened there is still fresh in many a memory. British intelligence was slow in persuading Churchill that Hitler was developing one of the secret weapons with the help of which he hoped to win the war. Thus it was not until the second half of 1943 that the Royal Air Force carried out the first of a series of raids against the rocket establishment. But by then the V-1, a small pilotless glide aircraft that was the prototype for the cruise missile of today, was already rolling off the production line, to be followed not long after—but fortunately too late to affect the outcome of the war—by the V-2, a true ballistic missile. Both weapons were used in attacks against England, the first V-1s being launched at London in daylight a week after the start of the Normandy invasion in June 1944. These small machines flew in at about a thousand feet until their engines cut out, leaving people below to wonder where they would land and explode. The first V-2s followed in September, unheralded (because supersonic), suddenly descending to wreak death and destruction with their 1,600-pound warheads. Several other types of rocket weapons were developed by both sides, mainly for use on the battlefield, but the V-1 and V-2 were the only relatively big ones that were used during the war.

By January of 1945, von Braun, sensing that he was on the losing side, decided to make his way to the American lines. Five hundred of his team, the best of the lot, together with all his records, went with him, and 115 soon settled in the United States. Only one German designer of note was left for the Russians to recruit. But as Grigory Tokady, a leading Russian rocketeer who later defected to the West, discovered, the Russians were not behind the Germans in ideas and theoretical knowledge. Stalin's purges of the 1930s had not deprived the Russian space programme of any of its leading lights. What had set it back was the over-running of western Russia in the early part of the war —and the fact that the Russian rocketeers had to turn their attention to more immediate problems of military research and development. The Russian weakness lay in their lack of technical expertise; after the war they decided to transfer to the USSR some hundreds of the lesser technical fry who had been part of von Braun's team. Seven years later, the Russians concluded that they had learned all they could from them, and most were repatriated to Germany.

Space technology entered the political arena after von Braun began work under US Army auspices to build more powerful rockets than the single-stage V-2. A bitter battle started between the Army, the Air Force, and the Navy to determine which was to lead the American space programme. The Russians avoided a similar dispute by establishing a single Department for Rocketry and Radar, which they provided with vast resources. New rocket ranges were built, and plans were immediately laid for the design of an intercontinental missile. Although the Russian aero-dynamicists and engineers, including such distinguished figures as A. N. Tupolev, had to work in 'gulags', everything that could be provided to further their work was theirs for the asking. By 1949 an improvement of the V-2 with a range of 550 miles was supplied to units of the Red Army. By 1952 an IRBM had been manufactured, and the Russian rocketeers were pressing on with the design of an ICBM, the one that in 1961 was to shoot Yuri Gagarin into space, and that was also able to carry the nuclear warheads that the Russians were already manufacturing.

More than anything else, it was the launching of Sputnik I in October 1957 that galvanized the space race. The whole world, and not just the United States, was startled. If the Russians could put an artificial satellite into space, they could deliver a nuclear warhead wherever they wanted. The American inter-service dispute had to be settled, and settled it was, by the usual kind of compromise. A civilian-led NASA was established, and each of the services was provided with a piece of the R&D pie with which to pursue its military concerns with space. It appeared, to a world worried by thoughts of nuclear war in space, that space technology was under civilian control. In fact the United States provided itself with a triad of nuclear forces (air-, land-, and sea-based) not because of a critical analysis of what was needed to establish an invulnerable deterrent, but because of service rivalry. Needless to say, the Russians were only too ready to follow suit and establish their own triad of strategic nuclear forces; for them the civil and military aspects of space had never been separated.

Almost alone among those of his countrymen who shaped public opinion, President Eisenhower was unbelieving and unmoved by cries that America was behind in space and in the arms race. Professor McDougall records the amazing range of figures that the three services were bandying around to whip up enthusiasm for their missile programmes. The Air Force declared that the USSR had deployed at least 300 ICBMs by 1960.

The Navy's figure was ten. The Army's and the CIA's estimate was 125 to 150, but after the reconnaissance satellite Samos 2 orbited the earth in January 1961, the figure was reduced to 60. A few months later, after further space reconnaissance, the figure became 'at most fourteen'. To help him judge which of the many much-vaunted ventures into the technological unknown was worth supporting—and for what reason—Eisenhower appointed a Presidential Science Adviser and a Science Advisory Committee.

Professor McDougall makes no mention of the fact that the post-Sputnik hysteria about the presumed technological superiority of the Soviets also resulted in a call for the mobilization of all the technical brains available to the West. In 1956, when the world was starting to worry about nuclear fallout and growing East-West tensions, the North Atlantic Council set up a small committee of foreign ministers to consider, among other matters, Allied cooperation in science and technology. A special task force under the chairmanship of Professor Joseph Koepfli of Caltech (at the time also scientific adviser to the State Department) was then convened to consider how this could best be done. Its deliberations—I was the British delegate—were made all the more urgent by the launching of Sputnik I, and our recommendation that a NATO Science Committee be set up was immediately accepted. The committee remains a highly successful and thriving institution, although it has never played a significant part in the short-term development of NATO's military strength.

Despite Eisenhower's scepticism, the 'missile gap'

became one of the major issues in the campaign that brought John F. Kennedy to the White House. Ironically, it was a myth that had been encouraged by Khrushchev and his generals, whose purpose was to secure whatever propaganda value they could from the Soviet Union's presumed superiority in space. As Professor McDougall puts it, 'Secrecy, the most potent weapon of the totalitarian state, permitted the deception and fed Western imaginations.' 'A strategy of deception, therefore, capitalized on Soviet strengths and cloaked Soviet weaknesses.'

Eisenhower's constant concern about the way secrecy exacerbated the mutual suspicions of the two superpowers, and so spurred the arms race, led him in 1956 to lay before the Russians his first 'Open Skies' proposal. They rejected it as a ploy. Early in 1957 he tabled at the UN General Assembly a further and more detailed proposal whereby 'future development in outer space would be directed exclusively to peaceful purposes and scientific purposes' by bringing 'the testing of [satellites and missiles] under international inspection and participation.' This offer was also rejected by Khrushchev. (So was his own, I seem to remember, when he suggested some years later that the United States and the Soviet Union should exchange the space photographs they were taking of each other's territory.) The net effect was that Eisenhower could not prevent the mid-1950s from becoming what Professor McDougall calls 'the most dynamic and imaginative years in the history of American military R&D. . . . Every space booster and every strategic missile in the American ar-

senal, prior to the Space Shuttle and the Trident sub-
marine-launched ballistic missile (SLBM) of the 1970s,
date from these years.' We need have no doubt that
the same thing was happening in the Soviet Union.

The fact is that neither side was prepared to take
the risk of being outdone by the other. Space surveillance of the Soviet Union was essential to the United
States. How otherwise could the American people be
satisfied that the USSR, which was adamantly opposed
to 'intrusive inspection', would not breach whatever
arms control agreement it might sign? Both sides were
testing ballistic missiles. Both were beginning to think
about the design of anti-satellite weapons, which they
realized would be a major threat also to the deployment
of reconnaissance and other kinds of spy satellites.
Weapons in space, moreover, would be a threat to other
nations, all of which had the right to deploy communications, meteorological, mapping, and navigational
satellites. Questions such as how far a nation's sovereign
'territory' extended into the sky, where 'space' began,
and whether the American satellites could lawfully
overfly Russian territory (and vice versa) had to be settled; and they were to some extent when it was agreed
that, as their major contributions to the International
Geophysical Year of 1957–58, both superpowers would
launch satellites for peaceful scientific observations.

The testing of nuclear weapons in space was foreclosed by the Partial Test Ban Treaty of the summer
of 1963. Later that year the United States and the Soviet
Union jointly agreed that neither would ever place nuclear weapons in orbit. This agreement was followed

by a 'Declaration of Legal Principles' governing the exploration and use of outer space, which in 1967 became enshrined in the UN Outer Space Treaty. This treaty, to which both superpowers were party, 'denuclearized' outer space; it also disallowed the militarization of the moon—an idea that had long been canvassed, and which indeed is still occasionally voiced by certain extraterrestrial warriors. A convention requiring the registration by the UN of all objects launched into space followed in 1976—but without any requirement that satellites should be examined by an international authority in order to determine their purpose.

With these quasi-legal niceties out of the way by the end of the 1960s, the superpowers proceeded with their separate space programmes, military and civil. Professor McDougall tells how President Kennedy's Science Adviser, Jerome Wiesner, as well as his entire Science Advisory Committee, were totally opposed to the Apollo man-on-the-moon project, and argued that the cost of this venture was altogether incommensurate with its possible scientific value. The President decided, however, that the project should go ahead for reasons of political prestige. He had another reason. By taking up slack in the aerospace industry, Apollo would reduce the pressure on the Defense Department to underwrite programmes that could not be justified strategically (for example, the ill-fated Skybolt). Once the decision was taken, Wiesner and his committee fully cooperated with NASA in deciding which of three possible methods of effecting a landing on the moon would be the safest and the best. Professor McDougall exaggerates somewhat when he writes that Wiesner and von Braun 'crossed swords' on the subject during the course of a presidential visit to Huntsville, Alabama, where a static test of the Saturn rocket had been arranged. I was fortunate to have been included in the party, and the discussion the reporters overheard and described as a confrontation simply revealed that it had not been decided whether it was best to land a man on the moon by way of a lunar module or by some other method. What they did not overhear was Harold Brown, then the Pentagon's Director of Defense Research and Engineering, remarking in a loud voice as von Braun was introducing half a dozen or so of his colleagues to the President, 'They haven't had so big a day since Hitler inspected them at Peenemünde.' Von Braun was probably too intent on his introductions to hear, but I remember hoping that the President did.

Professor McDougall does not ask whether the enormous cost of the Apollo programme was rewarded by any significant scientific gain, or whether the amazing courage of Neil Armstrong, who sent the message from the moon about a giant leap forward for mankind, had any lasting propaganda value. The Russians apparently did not have a man-on-the-moon programme. Not long after, however, they landed a radio-controlled moon-buggy, which automatically transmitted observations about the lunar surface. It even sent back to earth samples of lunar rock which, like those collected by the Apollo crews, very much resembled rocks on earth; these put to rest some speculation and provided an experimental basis for the refinement of the theory of lunar evolution. It is a moot point which feat was technically the more outstanding—automatic trans-shipment of lunar rock to the earth or bringing the samples back by hand. It is anybody's guess as to which deserves more prestige—a pedestrian or an automobilist on the moon.

Professor McDougall's narrative of events comes to an end at this point, when both the US and the USSR seemed content with the way things were going. Neither saw any merit in placing nuclear weapons, or indeed any weapons, in space, but both felt free to pursue their military reconnaissance and other programmes. Cooperation with other countries was of no interest to the Russians. To the Americans, 'competition was the motive force for space spending'. They were ready to cooperate for scientific purposes, but when it came to space engineering, commercial competition ruled. Professor McDougall records how many spacecraft were launched by both superpowers up to the start of the 1980s, and provides figures for their presumed expenditure on R&D, but he tells us far too little about the thriving space programmes of other countries, and nothing much about the series of Russian space stations (one crew of cosmonauts lived for nearly eight months in Salyut 7, which was serviced regularly by supply ships) or about the friendly exchanges that go between NASA and its opposite number in the Soviet Union, particularly in the study of biomedical problems. Sadly, too, there is no discussion of the impact of the bilateral ABM Treaty of 1972 on the politics of space, or any reference to its significance for President Reagan's Strategic Defense Initiative.

Instead we are constantly confronted by Professor

McDougall's deep and despairing concern about the impact of technology on political action, an issue that leads him to conclusions that I find somewhat dubious. His pessimism derives from what he senses will be the inevitable outcome if a country's technological effort is directed by its government, and what he predicts will be the consequences of what he calls 'command technology' and 'command innovation.' He defines command technology as 'the institutionalization of technological change for state purposes.' This came of age, he says, in World War II, when 'an evolutionary leap' occurred 'in the relationship of the state to the creation of new knowledge. Not only did the Soviets rethink and reaccelerate their R&D machinery in these years, but Western governments came to embrace the model of state-supported, perpetual technological revolution, create national infrastructures for such a program, and quintuple their funding for R&D in support of national goals.' No longer, writes Professor McDougall, did state and society merely adust to new 'tools and methods'; instead they 'took upon themselves the primary responsibility for generating new technology', with the consequence that not only the Soviet Union, which had 'reified the notion of centralized mobilization of science and technology in peacetime,' but all governments have become revolutionary. The Soviet Union, a Communist state, was always a technocracy, always in a race for technological superiority. The United States, a democracy, has had to become one.

Both of them, Professor McDougall tells us,

'derived political goals, be they obnoxious or benign, from some impulse or another, and then applied military technology to their achievement.' This process he is prepared to regard as 'excusable'. But he rejects as 'too terrible to entertain' the alternative notion—that in an age of nuclear weapons technological change can be an 'independent variable'. Still, when we reach the final chapter of the book, we find that Professor McDougall has become fearful both of 'command technology' *and of* technology as an independent variable. McDougall the historian has become McDougall the moralist, joining with those, like Bertrand Russell, Aldous Huxley, and Leo Tolstoy, who 'sensed the dark side of state-supported "invention of the future".' Finally, he also sees the day when science 'will have reached absolute limits in its quest for the origins, extent, composition, and fate of the material universe. When that day arrives,' so he writes, 'the technocratic pump may cavitate, the human heart have a meltdown, and science become again a branch of moral philosophy.' These are strange words to find at the end of a book that began by offering some hope that political choice could prevent technology from leading mankind into the abyss.

There are two issues in the argument that lead Professor McDougall to throw up his hands in despair at the thought that 'the unending race to keep up with foreign military and economic competition threatens to erode the very values that make one's society worth defending in the first place,' and which also lead him to predict that one day the methods of scientific inquiry will exhaust their value. The general question concerns the relation of society to technology and science, about which a vast literature exists; the more specific problem is the meaning and limits of what he calls 'command technology,' and the dependence or independence of technology as a variable that determines human affairs.

Let us look at the first question. Is it possible to separate the abstraction 'society' from the tools that are used by the individuals who constitute the society? The answer is clearly no if one has in mind the era when the craftsman reigned supreme, before factories were designed for the mass-production of goods. In those days the authority of organized society, in the form of the State had no need to 'command technology.' Technology was the very essence of society.

The pace of technological change accelerated sharply during the eighteenth and nineteenth centuries. This sometimes led to social unrest, but it did not take long, again, before those who had the money were eagerly demanding whatever fruits of new invention were regarded as desirable. Almost all the new mechanical contraptions of the industrial revolution were invented by individuals who were trying to find better ways of doing what was already being done. They had no formal scientific education, and most of them worked purely empirically. They were not commanded by anybody or anything.

It was at this stage that science started to come to the aid of technology, first by providing an understanding of some of its workings, and second, by the rapid rise in scientific experimentation and professionalism.

In turn, technology provided science with new tools with which to delve further into the unknown. Everything Professor McDougall writes about the enormous technological advances of the years since the end of World War II merely illustrates the power of modern engineering when allied, however remotely, to science. What is more, all these recent advances have become integrated into the fabric of society in basically the same way as the more mundane advances of an earlier industrial age. Any technological change that results in a presumed benefit, whether by reducing the burden of labour or the need for labour, or by adding to the pleasures or security of life, will be absorbed into the fabric of society—which, of course, becomes transformed in the process.

I seriously doubt that it matters to society at large which way technological change comes about—whether as a result of the inspiration of a lone inventor, or because of the spontaneous or contrived demand of the market, or in response to 'command technology,' either from the State or from, say, an international pharmaceutical company. It will, in any case, eventually be absorbed. The process of absorption may well cause domestic political difficulties, as old industry is forced to give way to new, as the labour cost of production declines. It may cause international difficulties, either because international trade is disturbed or because radio and television, by instantaneously making all parts of the world aware of new wealth-creating developments wherever they may occur, widen the political gulf between the haves and have-nots. It may mean, moreover, that some hidden social debt is being incurred because the new technology results in environmental damage. But the absorption of technology will nonetheless continue.

Technology itself will never automatically sound a warning against any of its deleterious effects, whether social or material (for example, the acid rain problem). Nor could technology itself generate an automatic warning that a war in space, or a war in which nuclear weapons were used, would be disastrous for mankind. In the end it is for society to decide whether technological change is for good or for bad.

I turn now to the more specific issue. How dependent or independent are significant discoveries in science and technology? The fact is that, while governmental 'command technology' can see to it that the material resources are there to encourage advances in particular directions, so-called 'break-throughs' cannot be commanded. Governments have tried to 'command' the design of an economic wide-bodied supersonic carrier aircraft with a range greater than that of the Concorde. The Concorde is still the best we have. The truth is that strokes of technological genius cannot be 'commanded.' They just happen. Great leaps in scientific understanding are even rarer. No one could have decreed that Alexander Fleming should transform all our lives by discovering penicillin, or that the chemical structure of the DNA molecule should be unravelled just when it was.

Not only are we always ignorant of the next major advance that may be made in scientific understanding;

we may, because of the prejudice of conventional belief, be blinding ourselves to some new scientific 'truth' that has already been discovered, or alternatively promoting what might turn out to be false. Mendel published his basic law of genetics in 1866, but despite his efforts to publicize his discovery it passed unnoticed until 1900. As I have already noted (p. 17), the classical and highly important kinetic theory of gases was elucidated in 1845 by Waterston, but the paper he submitted on the subject to the Royal Society was rejected.

Discovery may also be mistimed even when the climate for acceptance is totally favourable, which is what happened to Charles Babbage in the early nineteenth century (see p. 18). There are other examples of a similar kind.

In an age of nuclear weaponry, it may be disturbing to think of technological advances as 'independent variables'. Nonetheless, significant new scientific or technological knowledge will always be 'independent' at the moment it surfaces. It is the use that is made of new science or new technology, whether planned or unplanned, that becomes the dependent variable. If President Reagan supposes that some blinding new discoveries will be made in response to his plea to the scientific world to make the American people invulnerable to nuclear ballistic missiles, he is deluding himself. Of course it is conceivable that they might be. It is, however, more realistic to suppose that his 'technology command' is no more than a challenge to exploit to the greatest extent possible what basic knowledge already exists. But even if it ever proved possible to make a defence in space work perfectly, it would allow no time for human reason to influence the millisecond reactions of infra-red detectors and laser beams. There would be no place in it ironically, for presidents, secretaries of state, or generals. Technology would, to use Professor McDougall's phrase, really have come of age. A technological variable originally dependent on presidential command would have become independent.

I would judge that Professor McDougall's pessimism is due not so much to any worry about the institutionalization of science in the service of the State as it is to fears about the continuing arms-race. Eisenhower himself was more to the point in his farewell address. He knew that he had been unable to check the forces ranged against him by the armed services and by their opposite numbers in the USSR, and that in consequence he had failed to curb the arms-race. It was for that reason that he warned, as Professor McDougall reminds us, that

> the prospect of domination of the nation's scholars by Federal employment, project allocations, and the power of money is ever present—and is gravely to be regarded. . . . Yet in holding scientific research and discovery in respect, as we should, we must also be alert to the equal and opposite danger that public policy could itself become the captive of a scientific-technological élite.

We need to remember today that the élite to whom Eisenhower referred was made up of only those who had committed themselves to the mechanics of the arms-race and, to a lesser extent, to the race in space. There are probably more such people around today. But today, too, there is much more to science than defence and space, and far more élite science outside than inside the aerospace industries. The use of science in the service of the State is vital in the furtherance of public health and welfare, and in the regulation and monitoring of all public services. More than that, scientists are citizens of the State, and many of them are better able to see beyond the immediate technological horizon than can some politicians or generals who may be enjoying the power of command. The convergence of the United States and the Soviet Union has not meant that American scientists need fear the fate of a Sakharov. By being critical about the uses to which technology is put, they could help to see that we avoid at least some of the perilous rocks that lie in our path as we steer our way into the future.

REFERENCE

1. McDougall, Walter A., 1985, *The Heavens and the Earth: A Political History of the Space Age*, New York: Basic Books.

7

Presidents and Their Scientific Advisers

FROM PRESIDENT LINCOLN TO
PRESIDENT ROOSEVELT

Benjamin Franklin, the man who has been styled the Francis Bacon of the eighteenth century, had enormous faith in the power of scientific knowledge, and a strong belief that it would play a powerful part in the development of the country of which he was so distinguished a citizen. I doubt, however, if he could ever have imagined how much the America of today would owe to science for its pre-eminent position in the world. It was certainly not a debt that was deliberately incurred. The reality is that the search for gain infused the community of scientists as much as it did every other part of American society, and a widespread exploitation of technology was thus part and parcel of the process by which the economy of the United States expanded. Yet both the American Philosophical Society, which was founded at Franklin's instigation in Philadelphia in 1744, and the American Academy of Arts and Sciences which followed in Boston in 1780, were essentially learned societies designed on the European model.[1] Their main interest was the discussion and dissemination of new knowledge. There was no suggestion that either society should serve as an institution whereby the scientific activities of the country would be co-ordinated and directed, although in the memorandum in which, in 1743, he proposed the foundation of the Philosophical Society, Franklin had given the term 'useful knowledge' a very practical tinge. Nor was this task made a statutory responsibility of the National Academy of Sciences, the body that was established by Act of Congress in 1863 on the understanding, which was made clear from the start, that it could be called upon to 'investigate, examine, experiment and report upon any subjects of science or art demanded by Government'. For, as Professor Don K. Price has put it, 'the organization of the Academy was more suited to the purpose of providing honor to its members than advice to the government'.[2] The National Research Council also failed to serve the purpose of a central co-ordinating body. This again was not surprising since, like the Academy, it then derived its financial support mainly from private sources.

At the beginning of the Second World War President Roosevelt realised the need for such a body, and in 1940 therefore set up the National Defense Research Committee, which a year later he placed under the direction of the Office of Scientific Research and Development. To further the national interest, this was made part of the President's own Executive Office.

OSRD's director, Dr Bush, had no doubt that government must be concerned in the progress of science. Without considering the social and economic factors that were also involved in the process, he saw advances in science, when put to practical use, leading to 'more jobs, higher wages, shorter hours, and higher standards of living'. His proposals under the title *Science—the Endless Frontier*,[3] were submitted in the summer of 1945, but the form in which they were carried out was certainly not what he had had in mind. The organisation which President Truman and Congress allowed to be born in 1950 was a National Science Foundation which was essentially concerned only with the advancement of fundamental science.

Part of the trouble lay in the fact that while the OSRD was the premier directing body of the national scientific effort during the war years, it was far from being the biggest dispenser of federal funds for research and development. Both the Navy and the Army disposed of far more than it did. And in the five years that elapsed after Bush's plan was submitted, and before the National Science Foundation was set up, not only the military but also other branches of the executive machine continued to add to their power in the deployment of scientific and technical resources. The last thing they were therefore likely to do was surrender their independence to an organisation which Bush had conceived of as covering the whole range of national scientific activity—other than nuclear power. In any event, many who were drawn into the debate about the National Science Foundation were less concerned with the possible benefits of a centrally directed policy for science than they were with the fear that the Federal government was threatening the independence of the scientific community. The National Science Foundation's first director, Dr Alan Waterman, who before had been head of the Office of Naval Research, was not only averse to the idea that the new body should assume the task of evaluating the research programmes of the separate elements of the President's executive arm, but also to the notion that it should 'develop policy' for all research and development supported by the Federal government. So it was that the National Science Foundation became an institution which was concerned with the support of basic research, while the Department of Agriculture, the Public Health Service, the military and other departments of the government continued to cultivate those fields of research and development which were related to their executive domains. More than that—for a time the Office of Naval Research became a main supporter of scientific research not only in industry, but also in the universities, with the Army and Air Force tagging on valiantly behind.

EISENHOWER AND THE PRESIDENT'S SCIENCE COMMITTEE

By the time the Korean War began in 1950, the resources which the Federal government was devoting to science and its technological applications were so considerable that it had become all but illusory that the President, or indeed Congress, could exercise the kind of detailed control over what was done as they did in a general way over the economy as a whole. The net effect was that between 1950 and 1957 there was no central organisation within the Federal government which was able to pass judgement on interdepartmental and inter-service disputes about the volume of resources for research and development which each of them should command. Nor was there any central institution which in effect bridged the gap between, on the one hand, the President's office and the various executive departments of the central government, and on the other, the congressional committees whose responsibility it was to decide what resources should be voted the President for the discharge of his executive powers—a responsibility which implied a detailed knowledge of the various programmes on which the funds that were agreed would be spent. A part-time Science Advisory Committee which President Truman established in 1951 as an advisory body to the Office of Defense Mobilization had little power, but from 1952 onwards it was using its own initiative in considering problems of national defence, including air defence and rocketry.

With the launch of Sputnik, concern became widespread that the Soviet Union was winning at least a part of a technological arms-race. President Eisenhower sought the advice of the National Academy of Sciences and also summoned a meeting of the Science Advisory Committee of the Office of Defense Mobilization, then under the chairmanship of Professor Isidor Rabi. Professor Rabi advised President Eisenhower 'in the presence of the committee that what he needed was a man whom he liked', a science adviser 'who would be available full-time to work with him right in his office, to help by clarifying the scientific and techno-logical aspects of decisions which must be made from time to time. He would be a part of his brain, so to speak.' President Eisenhower accepted the advice and designated Dr James R. Killian as Presidential Science Adviser. A President's Science Advisory Committee (PSAC) was simultaneously established. In the same year, the NATO Science Committee was established, with Professor Rabi as my opposite number representing the United States.

Since those days there have been nine Presidential Science Advisers: Drs James R. Killian and George Kistiakowsky to President Eisenhower; Dr Jerome B. Wiesner to President Kennedy; Dr Donald F. Hornig to President Johnson; Drs Lee DuBridge and then Edward E. David to President Nixon; Dr H. Guyford Stever to President Ford; Dr Frank Press to President Carter; and Dr George A. Keyworth, whom President Reagan appointed in 1981 and who retired in 1985.

THE VOICES OF EXPERIENCE

One ex-president, in the person of Gerald Ford, a number of scientists who served on the President's Science Advisory Committee, certain staff members either of the President's Science Advisory Committee or of the Bureau of the Budget, two who have closely followed developments from the ringside, and all but two—Kistiakowsky and Keyworth—of those who have held the office of Presidential Science Adviser, have contributed to a volume entitled *Science Advice to the President*.[4] They give their views about the need for central advice in the United States on matters of national policy that are critically affected by scientific considerations, and about the desirability of co-ordinating Federal programmes on research and development—costing the nation some $40 billion (and projected to rise in 1986 to $50 billion). The story they tell is both fascinating and instructive, even if it is not always the same story.

Dr Rabi's view is that to be effective, there needs to be a very personal relationship between the President and his adviser. 'Since it's personal, the technical competence of the adviser is only part of his qualifications . . . there must be an impedance match between the President and his Science Adviser . . . the Science Adviser must know and understand the problems of the President as he sees them . . . the Science Adviser must try to be a part of the President's mind-set.' The importance of these requirements is borne out only too well in the testimony of those who have held the office, and in particular in a critical chapter contributed by Dr William G. Wells, a man who was able to keep watch on the scientific affairs of the White House from the vantage point of the congressional committees on which he served for fourteen years. According to him, Drs Killian and Kistiakowsky succeeded because they got on well with President Eisenhower and with the rest of the White House staff. 'They were part of the inner circle of Presidential advisers.' Dr Wiesner was highly effective with President Kennedy. In many areas related to science and technology, he 'spoke for the President'. Like Bush and J. B. Conant who, without being named presidential science advisers, served President Roosevelt, and Drs Killian and Kistiakowsky, Dr Wiesner understood the political aspects of science-advising, that presidential science advisers, like advisers in other fields, 'ply their trade in the highly competitive arena of palace politics'. What is more, Dr Wiesner's relationship to President Kennedy in no way suffered when his counsel was rejected. As Chief Scientific Adviser on Defence to the Government of the United Kingdom, and also as one of Prime Minister Macmillan's scientific advisers, I enjoyed the closest relations with Dr Wiesner. Both of us were involved in the negotiations which led up to the Partial Test Ban Treaty and, throughout the years up to the signing of the agreement in Moscow in 1963, we were of the same mind in arguing for a ban on all tests. But whatever President Kennedy's personal view of what should be the goal, he found it impossible to go further than a ban on atmospheric, space and oceanic tests. This difference did not, however, affect the relations between Dr Wiesner and his President.

UNUSED ADVISERS

But, as William Wells writes, when Lyndon Johnson became President, 'a watershed was crossed in terms of science advice and the Presidency'. Dr Wiesner's successors—Donald Hornig, Lee DuBridge, Edward

David and Guyford Stever—were not in the inner circle of the presidential advisers. This fact was borne in on me very forcibly on one occasion. I was one of the small party which Harold Wilson when Prime Minister took with him on a visit to President Johnson early in June 1967, a visit which, as Wilson relates in his memoirs,[5] was mainly concerned with the threat of imminent war in the Middle East, following President Nasser's move to close the Straits of Tiran to Israeli ships (this and the Vietnam War foreclosed any serious follow-up with the President of the discussion that Harold Wilson had had a short time before with President de Gaulle regarding nuclear co-operation with France). After the morning's talks in the White House, it had been intended that all would attend a grand luncheon that had been laid on at the British Embassy. Instead, President Johnson insisted that we all lunch at the White House. We were placed at four round tables, Harold Wilson, who was on the President's right, suggesting that I sit on the President's left. Towards the end of the meal, Wilson turned the conversation to the need for governmental action on environmental matters, and only then did the President remember that he had a Science Adviser. 'Where's Hornig', he called to an aide. 'Find Hornig.' Dr Hornig came in as we were having coffee; he had been told nothing about the purpose of the visit.

Dr Hornig makes no bones about the difference between his position as Science Adviser and that of Dr Wiesner. In the section which he contributes to the book he writes that he was not 'a part of, or even near to, the inner circle'—most of whose members 'weren't sure why there was a Science Adviser or where OST should fit in their scheme of things.' When Lee DuBridge succeeded Hornig on the change of the presidency, the position worsened. DuBridge, according to Wells, 'seemed not to appreciate the nature of the White House political arena'; he was 'too nice' to be a member of the Nixon White House, in the same way as Hornig was 'a "Mr Nice Guy" in the Johnson White House'. Dr Edward David, who succeeded DuBridge in the Nixon administration, had the 'inner toughness' to make a job of the appointment, but he arrived too late. By the time of the presidential election of 1972, Nixon and his top aides—by all accounts, Kissinger in particular—had decided that the post of Presidential Science Adviser, as well as the President's Science Advisory Committee, should be abolished. Dr Stever, the director of the National Science Foundation, for a time doubled as Science Adviser to President Ford, who resurrected the post, during his brief period as President.

When President Reagan took office in 1980 two other important changes had already taken place at the centre. In 1962, when Wiesner was the Presidential Science Adviser, the Office of Science and Technology (OST) was set up under Congressional authority in the Executive Office. Under Wiesner's direction it was charged with the task of co-ordinating and evaluating all Federal programmes in research and development. In this capacity—but in this capacity only—the central machinary for science and technology was made accountable to Congress. In 1973 President Nixon abolished the OST together with the rest of the scientific advisory apparatus he had inherited. Congress had also established a Federal Council for Science and Technology. This was not abolished by President Nixon, which, in effect, meant that a small part of the central scientific machine was kept ticking over when the main part was dismantled, but with control very much in the hands of the President's Office of Management and Budget. This latter body has the enormous responsibility of keeping under constant review the entire range of programmes and activities of the Federal Government, but is often attended by deputies rather than principals. In place of the OST, however, the Congress in 1975 established its own Office of Technology Assessment independently of the Executive Office.

What all this means was that even in the apparently becalmed days of Hornig and DuBridge, when they had little contact with the inner circle around the President, they were not sitting in their offices just twiddling their thumbs. They still had to try to discharge the responsibilities of the Office of Science and Technology. Its terms of reference were as broad as it is possible to imagine, including, for example, the task of reviewing and co-ordinating all major Federal activities in science and technology, maintaining good and close relations with the country's scientific and engineering communities, furthering science and technology throughout the country, and so on, a remit which was even further widened by a later Congressional Act of 1976. However little they had to do with the matters which were of immediate concern to the

President, all this was more than enough to keep the Presidential Science Advisers busy. Nonetheless, distance from the inner circle of advisers—and science advisers are only part of a whole band around the President—was the reason why the office of Presidential Science Adviser was for a time in abeyance.

In its early days, the President's Science Advisory Committee was a very powerful body. If not representative of the whole community of American scientists, it certainly included some of its most outstanding members. More than that, many had contributed greatly to the technological mastery which the United States had achieved during the war years. They were privy to secret information, and they were also independent in their views, even in matters relating to defence. Tensions not surprisingly began to develop between the science advisers and the administration. Many were outspoken in their opposition to the war in Vietnam. Most of those in the know held that the resources for research and development that were being devoted to devising an anti-ballistic missile system could achieve nothing of practical or political value. Some were vocal in their opposition to the concept of commercial supersonic transport aircraft. As individuals, but not as representatives of the unanimous view of PSAC, some testified to congressional committees in opposition to presidential policies.

To Presidents Johnson and Nixon this smacked of disloyalty.[6] What is interesting is that there had been no charge of disloyalty when Dr Wiesner's opinions on major matters of national policy had differed from his master's. Had Drs Hornig, DuBridge and David also belonged to the inner circle of the Presidents they served, I imagine that even had they been opposed to the prevailing presidential wisdom about some major issue, they too would have been more effective than they proved. After all, if views cannot differ in 'inner circles', where can they differ? But what was clearly not practical politics was allowing differences of judgement on major matters to be ventilated outside the family, for example, in the press or in congressional committees, particularly when the President may have been at loggerheads with those same committees.

THE NEED FOR INDEPENDENCE IN SCIENTIFIC ADVICE

The Office of Science and Technology was answerable to the Congress as well as to the President. The position of members of the President's Science Advisory Committee who, of course, were privy to the affairs of the Office of Science and Technology, was therefore highly sensitive *vis-à-vis* the Congress, even though their connection with the President was privileged and not subject to congressional enquiry. The experience of Dr Richard Garwin, who served for two four-year terms on the President's Science Advisory Committee and who was chairman of several of its standing and *ad hoc* panels—as well as having served for many years as a consultant and adviser to different branches of the executive and the legislature—makes this quite plain. 'The power of the PSAC', he writes, 'lay not in speaking to the President or in speaking *for* the President, but in acting on behalf of the President in gathering information for the preparation of its reports and the formulation of possible policy options. . . . The comparative advantage of the PSAC lay in being able to demand discussion with government departments, in having access to national security information which was not available outside the government, or in being acquainted with the concerns of the President or the imminence of programmatic decisions in order to provide a report which could be not only correct but influential.' He goes on to say, however, that while 'the White House staff certainly has a desire and duty to advance the President's programs . . . the President's science advisory organization has an important role to play in formulating and challenging of programs.'

Dr Garwin recognised that members of the President's Science Advisory Committee owed a loyalty to Congress as well as to the President. He had been chairman of a panel of the Office of Science and Technology established to consider various aspects of the programme to develop a commercial supersonic transport aircraft, and had been summoned to testify as an expert on the subject before a congressional committee. This he did, but against the views that had been publicly expressed by President Nixon, by whose staff his action was condemned. In assessing the situation a month after his congressional appearance, he wrote a letter to his colleagues, which included the statement:

No PSAC member (except the Chairman acting as Science Adviser or Director of OST) may speak on any issue of national interest, unless the PSAC is unanimous on that issue. If members were permitted or encouraged to speak in support of Administration policies, while dissenting members were forbidden to speak against, one of two inferences would be drawn—either PSAC would wrongly be assumed to be unanimous, or it would be presumed that those against were forbidden to speak. It might as well be made public knowledge that only those supporting the President's policy are allowed to speak, in which case I believe that new members, faced with this policy, would hesitate to join. It could be recognized that in the long run and for the security of our nation and of the democratic system, informed discussion by responsible individuals is in the national interest.

I find it impossible to disagree with the latter statement. Nor indeed was President Nixon consistent in his reaction to members of the President's Science Advisory Committee who publicly expressed views which were contrary to his own. Earlier on, and at Wiesner's request, DuBridge had asked the President whether Wiesner should resign from the advisory committee, with which he was still connected, as he proposed testifying to Congress in opposition to the Safeguard—antiballistic missile—system. On this occasion President Nixon accepted the situation.

Today it is not just this issue which would make it awkward, but certainly not impossible, to resurrect the system of the President's Science Advisory Committee. Following the Watergate scandal and President Nixon's resignation, the Freedom of Information Act became law. Except in matters which affect national security, and which therefore would have to be discussed in secret session, the meetings of the President's Science Advisory Committee and such panels as it were to set up, would have to be open to anyone who wished to attend. But obviously there would be enough matters that relate to national security to keep such a Council extremely busy—without being inhibited by the glare of publicity.

But there is another reason why the whole pattern of central scientific advice which was established by President Eisenhower would probably not work today. Up to the time America became deeply committed to the war in Vietnam, the first science advisers, like most members of the President's Science Advisory Committee, had been closely involved in the evolution of their country's military and nuclear programmes. Drs Kistiakowsky and Wiesner cooperated closely with Herbert York, the first Director of Defense Research and Engineering in the Department of Defense, and with his successor Dr Harold Brown, both of whom controlled more than half the total of Federal resources that went to research and development. But the President's advisers and other members of the President's Science Advisory Committee were indisputably senior to the men who controlled the budgets for research and development in governmental departments. They were also in close touch with the affairs of the Atomic Energy Commission, with the science adviser in the State Department, and with the director of technical intelligence

in the CIA. Dr Wiesner's advice had been followed in
the appointment of assistant secretaries for scientific
affairs in several departments of the government. In
certain matters relating to national security he, like his
predecessors, spoke with the authority of the presidency.
But Hornig and those who succeeded him were not so
fortunate. As the war in Vietnam and the cold war with
the Soviet Union intensified, the resources for research
and development which the Pentagon commanded increased enormously. Finally Dr Kissinger, first in his
position as director of President Nixon's National Security Council, and then as Secretary of State, decided
that he on his own was competent to judge the technical
matters that related to the SALT negotiations. Unlike
President Kennedy when he was wrestling with the
problem of a test ban treaty, he felt no need to call on
the advice of a presidential science adviser or of a President's Science Advisory Committee. And when President Carter appointed Dr Frank Press to the post of
Science Adviser, he felt that there was no need for him
to cover the same ground as his Secretary for Defense,
Harold Brown, a man whose experience, first in one
of America's two nuclear weapons laboratories, then in
charge of research and development in the Department
of Defense, and finally as Secretary of the Air Force,
had fitted him admirably for the post he was filling.

THE FUTURE

So what of the future? Writing in 1980, Dr Willis
Shapley, who for many years was a senior official in

the Bureau of the Budget, and mainly concerned with research and development, and who was also a deputy administrator of the National Aeronautics and Space Administration (NASA), is well worth reading on the subject. He is at one with others who emphasise that the effectiveness of any central organisation depends on the way 'the Science Adviser fits into the structure of the Executive Office and the operating patterns of the Presidency'. Another major consideration is 'how the Science Adviser and his office relate to the rest of the Federal science and technology establishment'. In his view, 'the goal should be a minimal Science Adviser's office in the Executive Office supported by a heftier "Agency for Science and Technology" which, in addition, would perform central planning and leadership functions and bring together a group of federal agencies directly concerned with science and technology'. What is important is that the Office of Science and Technology Policy should work well with the Office of Management and Budget and that it should be 'accepted as a responsible partner in the decision process, rather than regarded with suspicion as a special pleader for science and technology'.

Dr Shapley then goes on to argue that even when successfully led by Frank Press for President Carter, the Office of Science and Technology Policy as then constituted could not:

fully meet the needs of the Executive Branch for central leadership on science and technology. The job is too big for a staff office in

the White House. There is a need for dealing
with more than just the most pressing atten-
tion-demanding problems. Leadership should
be available when needed on small policy
problems as well as great. The whole area of
the management of Federal R&D, technical
operations and services, cries out for more
leadership attention. There should be time to
think, to anticipate future problems, and to
try to get ahead of them. Decisions should
be based on a depth of understanding unlikely
to be achieved when the pace is so hectic. A
small, dedicated, but over-worked staff may
be able to put on one virtuoso performance
after another, but it cannot be expected to do
the full advisory and leadership job that Federal science and technology activities require.

He then continues:

The most critical shortcoming of the current
OSTP concept is that it fails to provide institutional continuity for science and technology advice in the Executive Office and
policy leadership in the Executive Branch.
The present arrangement is inherently unsta-
ble. It depends on personal understandings
among the principals in the Executive Office
and on the acceptance of OSTP by the other
bureaucracies there entrenched. All this could
vanish with a change in administration or

even a change in some key individuals. No one will deny a President the right to organize, staff, and operate his own office as he and his closest associates see fit. The same reasons that first pointed the Carter administration in the direction of abolishing OSTP, or at least removing it from the Executive Office, might well be persuasive to another President. Even if the shell of an OSTP survived, nothing would be easier than to ignore it if it is not wanted as a part of the official family. We have been down that road before. Institutional continuity is important for science and technology policy and leadership. The impact of science and technology is a long-term affair. Lead times are long. Studies of important topics can take many months to set up properly, months or perhaps years to conduct, and as long again to evaluate and implement; the whole process often stretches from one administration to the next. Each administration should not have to start from scratch. An institutional memory can help it to learn from past experiences and avoid unnecessary replowing of old ground.

Shapley's prescription to put all this right is to establish a permanent independent agency headed by a presidential appointee of cabinet rank, 'with broad central responsibilities for advice and leadership in science and technology in the Executive Branch'. Those agencies 'not integral to the missions of other departments would . . . become operating elements within the new agency' (e.g., NASA, the NSF, the National Bureau of Standards). The director would not 'control' the scientific and technological activities of other Federal agencies—such as Defense—but would be able to influence them as a member of the cabinet. But the director of the new agency would not be the President's Science Adviser. For the President's Science Adviser would be the 'personal adviser at the White House, a second independent voice when wanted', and drawing on the new agency—which, in effect, is what Vannevar Bush outlined for the national science foundation that never was—for technical and other support.

It all sounds very reasonable, if it could be made to work; that is to say, if the new body could take over such powerful bodies as the National Aeronautics and Space Administration without generating too much friction.

The formal and dual machinery suggested by Dr Shapley is difficult to imagine; the question is, would it work? Apparently Dr Keyworth, whom President Reagan appointed, was asked whether it could. We do not yet know whether he examined the question, and if he did, what conclusions he drew. He is reported as having said that 'he would not be funneling the ideas and sentiments of science into the administration as other presidential science advisers have done. "The desire of this administration is to have an adviser with scientific background . . . rather than a lobbyist or advocate for science. . . . Science and technology underlie probably a majority of problems facing the government, so they want a science adviser as a member of a policy-making team".[7] Dr Keyworth did establish a White House Science Council but, as noted on pages 88–89, neither he nor the Council was consulted by the President before he announced his SDI.

To operate effectively, and to command the respect of the vast body of American scientists, a presidential science adviser has to reveal the same personal authority in dealing with the host of problems that experience shows will need to be tackled as did the first three or four of the series of men whom he would be following. It is not a case of worrying about 'the ideas and sentiments of science' whatever Dr Keyworth intended by the phrase, but of recognising that short-term vested interests plague the life of the political leader. The chief scientific adviser has to learn to recognise them and, when necessary and possible and in the longer-term national interest, to rise above them. Dr Keyworth, who left the White House for a business consultancy, is mainly known for his passionate support of President Reagan's SDI.

The United States, of course, is not the only industrial country in which the problem of scientific advice at the centre of government is a matter of concern. Germany has a ministry of technology. The one in France, which was presumably concerned mainly with the allocation of funds either to scientific institutions or to projects in research and development, whether in governmental establishments or industry, has recently been dismantled. (The French President, M. Mitterrand, also appointed a personal scientific adviser.) In the Soviet Union the pattern is very different, since many members of the government, in particular the heads of departments of the very powerful state committee for science and industry, are scientists or engineers. In the United Kingdom, the position of Chief Scientific Adviser to the government was abolished some 12 years ago, and a Select Committee of the House of Lords is now enquiring into the whole network of scientific advice to government, with particular reference to advice and co-ordination at the centre.

Clearly the same administrative pattern for the provision of scientific advice at the centre cannot apply in all countries. Constitutional differences in the structure of governments would make this impossible. Nonetheless, the need will always have some common features, all deriving from the basic fact that, whatever its nature, central government is responsible for all that is done in its name. A president or prime minister cannot be expected to find the time to keep informed about all that is going on over the entire range of research and development, nor to anticipate which political decisions are likely to be conditioned by scientific considerations, present or future. In 1972, Harold Macmillan wrote, with reference to defence matters:

> In all these affairs Prime Ministers, Ministers
> of Defence and Cabinets are under a great
> handicap. The technicalities and uncertainties of the sophisticated weapons which they

have to authorise are out of the range of normal experience. There is today a far greater
gap between their own knowledge and the
expert advice which they receive than there
has ever been in the history of war.[8]

This is still true today.

Obviously governments can go on muddling along
without a source of scientific advice at the centre or
without any machinery to co-ordinate their scientific
and technological activities. But if and however such
a source is created, together with the necessary administrative apparatus, it must have the authority to do its
job, whatever its nature. It must have access to whatever
information it wants about the activities of those governmental departments which engage in scientific and
technological work. Ideally its responsibilities should
never be divided; for example, major fields of activity,
such as the nuclear, should not be outside the orbit of
its review. And above all it must be led by men who
are respected by their political masters, not just because
of their scientific eminence, but because of their sen-
sitivity to the political problems of central government,
at the same time as the appointed advisers are respected
by the scientific community for their scientific knowledge and objectivity. This may be calling for a great
deal; but in these dangerous days that is what is necessary. To ask for less is an invitation to failure. There
have been enough wasteful exercises in the setting up
of makeshift and inevitably temporary administrative
organisations.

REFERENCES

1. Price, Don K., 1965, *The Scientific Estate*, Cambridge, Mass.: Belknap Press of Harvard University Press.
2. Price, Don K., 1954, *Government and Science*, New York: New York University Press.
3. Bush, Vannevar, 1946, *Endless Horizons*, Washington, D.C.: Public Affairs Press, and 1945, *Science—The Endless Frontier: A Report to the President*, Washington, D.C.: U.S. Government Printing Office.
4. Golden, William T. (ed), 1980, *Science Advice to the President*, Oxford: Pergamon.
5. Wilson, Harold, 1971, *The Labour Government 1964–1970: A Personal Record*, London: Weidenfeld & Nicolson and Michael Joseph.
6. Dr James Schlesinger, a former Director of the CIA, was Defense Secretary in the mid-seventies under two Republican Presidents. He is a life-long republican, and most recently he served on President Reagan's MX missile commission, but despite his impeccable conservative credentials on defence, Schlesinger does not share the President's Star Wars dream. He has recently said (BBC TV programme, *This Week Next Week*, February 16, 1986) that 'support for Star Wars has become a kind of loyalty test within the Administration, and if there are those who are not true believers, they had better keep their scepticism hidden. It has become very difficult to raise questions about the validity of Star Wars.'
7. *International Herald Tribune*, May 1981.
8. Macmillan, Harold, 1972, *Pointing the Way*, London: Macmillan, p. 250.

8
Scientists, Bureaucrats and Ministers in the UK

MINISTERS AND BUREAUCRATS

New governments assume office with fairly clear ideas about the legislative programme on which they will need to embark in fulfilling the promises they will have made to an electorate that was persuaded to throw out their predecessors. Sometimes they also have ideas about changes in the 'machinery of government' which, in their view, will be either needed or desirable in achieving their objectives. New departments may be created and old ones abolished. Responsibilities may be shifted from one Ministry to another. Despite the presumed political neutrality of the Civil Service, the permanent head of a Department may on occasion be moved. And it is always easy for those who govern to believe that they could achieve more than they in fact do if only they had a better bureaucratic machine with which to work.

It is not only governments that worry about imperfections in the machinery of government. The issue often becomes the subject of public debate, such as the one triggered by Sir John Hoskyns after his retirement in April 1982 from the post of 'special policy adviser' to the Prime Minister, and to which Sir Douglas Wass, the outgoing head of the Treasury, forcibly contributed in the 1983 Reith Lectures.[1]

Sir John came to No 10 from industry. Three years of Whitehall left him with a poor impression of the higher British Civil Service which, in his view, is made up of a body of officials who have been conditioned by the steady decline in Britain's fortunes to a chronically pessimistic approach to any suggestion of change. Nonetheless, because they are there, they are the ones who 'shape' our ministers. As he points out, there is 'no staff college or alternative government in which ministers can learn their trade, nor is there any solid and coherent corpus of knowledge or method for them to master'.[2] It is the old story. The top layer of civil servants are hide-bound in the way they operate and they are incapable of providing their masters with clear ideas about ways of implementing the government's basic strategies, in particular, the prime goal of achieving financial stability. What is more, the Whitehall machine fails to set objectives for the departmental ministers who, in addition, lead impossible lives because of the mass of work they have to do, the papers they have to read, and the meetings they have to attend— all of which leave them no time to think for themselves.

It is too early to predict how the vigorous debate which Sir John instigated is going to end, whether it will just fade away or lead to yet another review of the Civil Service. There are many who feel that the picture which he has painted is too gloomy, and in particular that he has failed to understand the *political* dimension of government. Sir Douglas Wass has spelt out his reservations. Of course life was easier for ministers in the days before government had assumed the multifarious executive functions which it has taken on since the end of the Second World War. Lord Samuel—Sir Herbert Samuel as he was—once described to me how he was introduced to his first ministerial office as Postmaster General in Mr Asquith's Government of 1908–1910. He was greeted with great ceremony by his Permanent Secretary and a group of senior officials, and led to his spacious office, which he duly admired. His Permanent Secretary then remarked, 'I don't think, Postmaster General, that you need find the job too strenuous. Every Friday we lay round this conference table the papers that need your signature. Your predecessor found it quite easy. Indeed he was often able to do what was wanted so speedily that he did not even need to remove his hat.' Those were the days of silk hats and frock coats.

I have known Whitehall uninterruptedly and, I would say, fairly intimately for some forty years, most of the time as an 'amateur', serving on committees and advisory councils, but for twelve in a full-time capacity. It has certainly undergone many changes during the time I have known it, but my own belief is that all ministers still have the time—if that were all that was needed—to see that their departmental responsibilities

are discharged in ways which do not confound what
Sir John Hoskyns calls the government's basic strategic
policies and objectives—and which constitutionally it
is the government's business, not that of civil servants,
to define. Sometimes it may not prove possible to reconcile departmental with the government's basic strategic policies, and the latter, conceived at the outset
without a clear knowledge of the difficulties, may have
to change. Sometimes a minister may not be up to the
job that he has been given. On the other hand, permanent secretaries and those below them will be aware
of what an incoming government will try to achieve
without waiting to be handed a new set of instructions.
They will also be aware of the extent to which existing
commitments can obstruct new political objectives. It
is the business of civil servants to help their political
masters reconcile, so far as possible, their responsibilities with the prevailing realities. Indeed it is their duty
to warn ministers of the best way to avert difficulties in
bringing about change. Of course misunderstandings
between ministers and top civil servants sometimes occur; of course civil servants who have been moulded
by past experience may think that the objectives of new
ministers are misguided; and of course bureaucratic
procedures tend to become hallowed with time, and to
drive thought into ever-deepening ruts.

Success in concerting the activities of the Departments of government depends in the end on the
mutual trust and understanding in a cabinet over which
a Prime Minister presides as *primus inter pares*. If ministers are hard-pressed in their departmental duties, the
PM is even more so. It is not just the responsibility of

'Number Ten' to see that the government's departmental policies are coherent, and that they present an understandable picture to the public. As we know all too well, the centre of government has to react quickly to sudden and frequently dangerous contingencies. The question whether a Prime Minister's coordinating responsibilities would be more easily discharged were there a new central 'Department' is also an intermittent topic of public debate. My own view is that if such a Department were formed, it would not necessarily imbue a Prime Minister with authority were that quality not already there. Indeed, if a Prime Minister lacked authority over his or her cabinet colleagues, a prime-ministerial department could well become a source of friction between a central body of bureaucrats and their colleagues in Departments, and worse, a source of diversion from the main prime-ministerial responsibility for leadership and coordination. There are ways other than a new prime-ministerial office to help a cabinet that has to operate, not as a collection of ministers each fighting his own departmental corner, but as a body that epitomises loyalty to the principle of shared governmental responsibility. In the final analysis, personal relationships of politicians with each other and with their advisers determine the smoothness of the operations of government.

SCIENTISTS IN THE MACHINE

Shortly after Harold Wilson took office as Prime Minister in October of 1964, he set up a committee under Lord Fulton to 'examine the structure, recruitment and management, including training, of the Home Civil Service'. One of its main concerns was the same issue that Sir John Hoskyns has highlighted—namely the fact that the members of that section of the higher Civil Service which is most concerned in the formulation of government policy—the administrative class—as a rule have little specialised knowledge, have never worked outside the bureaucratic machine, and have too little 'contact with the community it is there to serve'. In contrast, the members of the Scientific Civil Service (and of other specialised groups of public servant) as a rule neither come into direct contact with the policy makers nor enjoy the preferments of promotions and honours that are the lot of administrative civil servants. As the Fulton Committee put it, 'scientists, engineers and members of other specialist classes are frequently given neither the full responsibilities and opportunities nor the corresponding authority they ought to have'.[3] One of Fulton's recommendations was that there should be both fewer classes and more movement in the public service, and that the barriers which separate the scientific civil servants from the administrative class, particularly at the higher levels, should be broken down in order to allow of interchange—and in particular to ease the path of scientists to the highest positions of departmental authority. Another recommendation, which was implemented in November of 1968, was that a Civil Service Department should be set up in its own right. This Department survived until 1981, when it was dissolved by the present Prime Minister, with its responsibilities for personnel management in the Civil

Service being handed over to the Secretary of the Cabinet and to the permanent head of the Treasury. The offices of Secretary of the Cabinet, of Head of the Treasury, and of Head of the British Civil Service, have been combined and separated more than once since the end of the Second World War. There may have been many reasons for the recent change, but one was clearly the Prime Minister's wish to reduce the number of government employees. It is said that Britain still has far more civil servants per head of population than any other country in Western Europe—something like one to nine.

That charge or, as it is sometimes regarded, that complaint, of course relates to all public servants— from the Secretary of the Cabinet at the top to the postman below. The administrative class, which is the target of Sir John Hoskyns' criticisms, numbers no more than some 3,000 highly intelligent men and women who decided to make non-electoral politics their professional career. Before the Fulton Committee started its deliberations, I had been designated by the Prime Minister 'Head of the Scientific Civil Service'—the only official ever to be so styled publicly. I cannot recall any special duties the title entailed, but in those days it was said that there were about 10,000 scientific to the 3,000 administrative civil servants.

Government scientists have been the subject of critical enquiry far more frequently than their administrative colleagues. I say 'more frequently' advisedly. Reports on one or other aspect of the place of science in the machinery of British government have appeared

on average at least once every five years since the end
of the Second World War. The most recent, in 1981,
came from the House of Lords' Select Committee on
Science and Technology.[4] Nobody ever seems satisfied
with the way scientists operate in government. Basically
the complaint, whether justified or not, remains the
same. At a time when the work of most departments is
conditioned by scientific and technical considerations,
scientists do not play the part they should, or could, in
a government's decisions on policy.

Because ministers and administrative civil servants
need to be kept aware of technical developments in the
fields of knowledge that affect their responsibilities, Departments, with few exceptions, necessarily have to employ scientists who must, or should, maintain close
links with the research councils and the universities.
Some Departments also have their own research establishments. Scientific considerations are of constant concern in Ministries such as Health, Agriculture, Energy,
Defence, and the Environment. In some Departments
they have an enormous and immediate impact on policy. For example, the wise application of new scientific
knowledge has improved British agriculture increasingly and steadily since the end of the Second World
War. Science, one might say, is so much ingrained in
the workings of the Department, that there is no more
need for the Minister to convene regular meetings with
his scientific officials than there would be point in asking them to set prices for wheat and pig-meat, or to
help sort out the Government's difficulties arising from
the Common Market's Agricultural Policy or from its

dealings with the National Farmers' Union. Every now and then some new political issue might blow up which would demand urgent scientific action—say, for example, adverse public reaction to the use of a new pesticide. But provided bureaucrats and scientists work together, the latter can in general leave it to the former to see that scientific considerations are not lost sight of in the mass of other factors that determine government policy.

The Department of Health and Social Security—at any rate the Health part—follows much the same pattern as Agriculture in the relationship of administrators and medical men. The 1946 decision to create a National Health Service was a political one, in which members of the medical profession played no more of a part than did the ordinary citizen. Indeed, many of them were deeply opposed to the Government's move. Once formed, however, the Department's Chief Medical Officer and his staff had more to say about the organisation of the NHS than did their administrative colleagues, whose main business it was to arrange the financial framework for the new service. It was and remains the medical man's responsibility—not the administrator's—to assure the safety of the drugs that are licensed, to decide what building and equipment needs to be provided for the doctors and, in concert with their colleagues, to agree on orders of priority within the financial limits set by the government as a whole.

The problem of marrying governmental policies to the best scientific knowledge is much more troublesome in Departments such as Energy or Defence, whose activities are sharply affected by technologies that change more rapidly than those in, for example, the farming world. There is also the basic difficulty that specialists often disagree about what is the best technical course to pursue in dealing with some particular problem. The disputes about the advantages of gas-cooled as compared with water-cooled nuclear reactors, or about, say, which type of water-cooled reactor to choose, are one obvious case in point. In addition there is always a danger that government policy can be distorted by technical dogma that has become impervious to change in the face of new facts or new understanding. Industrial interests may also be involved in the technical debate, and industry has its own vested and competitive interests. The public may be concerned about related—or even unrelated—environmental issues that are raised by technical developments. How is the bureaucrat or minister to decide what course to pursue? Few, if indeed any, ministers are active scientists. In deciding what to do, they have willy-nilly to take advice from their scientific staffs, sometimes directly, but far more frequently through discussion with the senior officials of their Departments—who, through their own political experience, or prejudices, may have their own views about the technical argument, and be better aware of public reactions than the scientists.

The general view is that ministers today *prefer* to obtain scientific advice indirectly from their top administrative officials. As the Lords' Select Committee on Science and Technology put it: 'The provision of scientific advice to Government, at least as regards day-to-day matters, is mostly the provision of advice to senior civil servants.' According to this committee, 'generalist' civil servants are not only the ones who advise ministers and formulate policy, but they are also in charge of the government machine and exercise financial control. The same charge, which Fulton and others before him made, has recently been repeated by the Council for Science and Society.[5] But some of Fulton's recommendations about breaking down barriers between the administrative and scientific civil servants have been implemented. Has something gone wrong since?

SCIENTISTS AND POLITICAL CHANGE

I suppose that any one of us could write down a list of what we consider the most important changes in government policy that have occurred since the end of the Second World War. Let me suggest a few. In the first post-war government we had a programme of university expansion, with particular reference to scientific manpower; a programme of nationalisation of various industries; a number of measures that we group together in the concept of a Welfare State, in particular, the creation of the National Health Service. In 1947 there was the secret decision that Britain would make her own nuclear weapons. 1948 and 1949 were the years of the Brussels Pact and the formation of NATO. In 1951 the Churchill Government that succeeded Attlee's second administration decided to denationalise steel and road transport, and to reduce defence expenditure below the level projected in Hugh Gaitskell's final budget. In 1956 the Government of the day decided to use force to settle the Suez problem. At the end of the 1950s we had the 'wind of change'—of decolonisation and of other measures to end Empire. 1973 saw our entry into the EEC. And today, the Government is trying to reduce the size of the public sector, and is taking unprecedented political risks as a consequence of its financial policies—in particular by tolerating a very high level of unemployment.

This list is an arbitrary one, but what I have set down is enough to provide a basis for my next question: what part did scientists—either in or out of government—play in the discussions that led to the changes in policy that were concerned? Except in the case of the universities and the nuclear weapon, my guess is very little or none. I also feel that *as scientists* they had no contribution to make. The issues were almost wholly political, and while bureaucrats, as administrators, had to do the hard work necessary to implement the relevant governmental decisions, they did not decide them. I well remember that the Treasury official who had the arduous task of organising the nationalisation of the iron and steel industry during Attlee's administration was then given the job of denationalising the embryonic state-controlled industry when Churchill's Government returned to power in 1951.

As I have said, apart from the nuclear bomb and the expansion of the universities, it is my view that scientists as such had no part to play in the decisions which resulted in my list of political milestones. Two questions then follow. The first is: *could* scientists have played a part, and if so, how? The second is: *should* they have played a part? My answer to both questions has to be equivocal. If professionally trained scientists had happened to be members of the government when the decisions were taken and, more so, of that part of government which constitutes the Cabinet, they would *ipso facto* have shared the responsibility for what emerged as major government policy. A few scientists have held ministerial office. The first was Lyon Playfair, who became Postmaster General in 1873. The second was Lord Salisbury, an amateur chemist and physicist who, before he became Lord Privy Seal, was Under-Secretary for Foreign Affairs between 1900 and 1903. The third was Lord Addison, a professor of anatomy who, having entered politics as a Liberal, in 1916 became a Cabinet Minister in Asquith's Government, and many years later, in 1945, when he had joined the Labour Party, a member of Mr Attlee's Government. There have been a handful of others, among them Lord Cherwell, the physicist who served both in Winston Churchill's wartime Cabinet, and in his 1951 administration; Sir John Anderson (later Lord Waverley), who was also a member of the wartime Cabinet; and Lord Peart, Minister of Agriculture in Harold Wilson's two administrations. Today's Prime Minister, Mrs Thatcher, is by professional training a chemist.

But my question is not so much directed at the extremely small number of men and women who in their university days read some branch of science, and who subsequently became members of the government, as it is at the scientific class of the bureaucracy and at members of scientific advisory councils. Could they, any more than their administrative civil service colleagues, have played a part? My answer is again, 'No'. For example, the belief that 'the means of production' should be in the hands of 'the people', is a basic tenet of socialist philosophy. It does not derive from, nor need derive from, any scientific analysis, any more than did the various measures that together add up to what we now call the Welfare State. If there were scientists who encouraged the political leaders who were responsible for bringing about legislation in the fields I have arbitrarily listed, they did so as men or women who were committed to the same social and economic purposes as the politicians who were in the front line of decision. If, for example, Lord Cherwell was among those who encouraged Winston Churchill in 1951 to denationalise steel and road transport, he did so not because he was a scientist, but because he was politically convinced that undoing some of the work of Attlee's Government was the right thing to do.

Apart from the two issues that I have singled out, and with which I shall deal separately, *should* scientists have played a part in the issues that I have listed? I can see only one where scientific prescience might have helped; namely, in the establishment of the National Health Service.

Because of its likely cost, Churchill's wartime Government was lukewarm about the idea of creating a National Health Service of the kind suggested in the 1942 Beveridge Report on Social Insurance and Allied

Services.[6] Attlee's post-war Government thought differently, and in 1948, Aneurin Bevan, Minister of Health, introduced the service we now have as a measure which gave real meaning to the concept of social justice. The prevailing belief was that there was a reservoir of medical care that could be distributed among the population in accordance with need, and not as commanded by personal wealth. But priorities in the field of public expenditure soon began to obtrude. Towards the premature end of Attlee's second administration, the cost of the armed services pressed hard on the Chancellor's budget, and Bevan found himself differing sharply from most of his colleagues in the assignment of national priorities. A relatively small cut in NHS expenditure was proposed, with the press focusing on a small charge which was going to be made for false teeth and spectacles. The cut had little meaning except as a token move against Bevan and the Service that he had created. He resigned.

Bevan was served by a first-rate Chief Medical Officer, Sir Wilson Jameson, who kept in close touch with the leaders of the profession and with the Medical Research Council. Between them, what was emerging from the medical research laboratories and clinics must surely have been known. Yet, at the time, no one seemed to see, or imagine, the fabulous advances in medical science that were going to be made in the ensuing three decades. Nor was there much, if indeed any talk then about the likely increase in the numbers of old people in the population. Had Jameson or some other medical leader been a reliable prophet, he might have told Bevan that in the long run, the inevitable consequence would be a great increase in the demand for increasingly costly medical practice and of more aid to the elderly, and that some braking system on medical demand would need to be devised. It took every bit of ten more years before the immense pressure that social demand would exert on medical resources became apparent. Indeed, this was not explained to the public until 1966, when Enoch Powell published a brilliant tract on medicine and politics.[7] Today we are faced with the stark realisation that in its present economic state, the country cannot afford the medical service it would like. As I have said, a prescient medical scientist might have seen at least part of this at the start—but to the best of my knowledge, there was not one around.

THE UNIVERSITIES AND SCIENTIFIC MANPOWER

The first of my two examples of major governmental policy in which scientists did play a part is straightforward. It was the decision of the post-war Attlee Government to expand the size of the universities so as to double the output of scientists and engineers as rapidly as possible.

Trained technical people had been in short supply throughout the war, and it was known that shortages would continue into the period of post-war reconstruction. The recommendation[8] to expand the universities came from a small committee chaired by Sir Alan Barlow, then the Second Secretary of the Treasury, and the majority of whose members were scientists. It was accepted, and the phase of university expansion that followed was administered by the University Grants Committee, and monitored by the Scientific Manpower Committee of the Advisory Council on Scientific Policy, a body that was set up by the Government in January of 1947, following yet another recommendation of the Barlow Committee. Until 1963, the universities grew at a steady pace. Then the Government's acceptance of a recommendation[9] of a committee under Lord Robbins led to an explosive growth in higher education triggered mainly by the broad principle that the state should provide a university education (or its equivalent) for all who had the requisite 'entry requirements' and who wished to continue with their education. As we know only too well from the 'cut-back' which the universities are now suffering, 'demand' in due course again outran resources.

It is often suggested that the Robbins Committee went too far. Given, however, that political considerations determined the acceptance of its recommendations, I do not think that any blame for the present cutback in university finances can be laid either on the scientists who were on the Committee, on the UGC or, for that matter, and in the years since Robbins reported, on any scientists who were either in the upper reaches of the bureaucracy or members of official advisory bodies.

I must, however, confess that I had my doubts. As Chairman of the Scientific Manpower Committee I was asked to appear before the Robbins Committee, by whom I was cross-examined about the successive and different statistical procedures which we had used in making our estimates for the future demand for scientific manpower. I made it plain that I held no brief for any of them, and that had my committee decided to make yet another estimate, we would no doubt have devised another way of doing so.[10]

Given no workable braking system, it was inevitable that the demand for higher education would exert very heavy pressure on resources. Yet, however close his or her personal relations with the Prime Minister or with cabinet ministers, it is my view that no doubting scientist could have persuaded Lord Home's government to be cautious about the Robbins' recommendations. Like the health service, a 'social good' was involved. Rejecting the Robbins Report would have turned it into an electoral issue, and would have added to all the other factors which brought about the Government's defeat at the election which took place less than a year after the Committee reported. More than that, I do not think that the situation of the universities today would be any different from what it is if every permanent secretary who had been concerned during the period of university expansion, and now of contraction, had come from the scientific as opposed to the administrative class of the civil service. One of them did.

THE NUCLEAR DECISION

If no clear lessons for the scientific policy-maker can be drawn from the story of university expansion, they certainly can from that of Attlee's decision to develop a nuclear bomb, a story the details of which are no longer secret, but of which only a brief account can be given here.

When he became Prime Minister at the end of July 1945, Attlee was ignorant both about Tube Alloys, Britain's nuclear organisation, and about the Manhattan Project, the codename for the vast American nuclear programme. At the Potsdam Conference of mid-July 1945, President Truman told him (in writing!) that the Americans were going to drop an atom bomb on Japan. Attlee's belief that an atom bomb merely implied some devastating new explosive of the kind which the world already knew was quickly shattered. On 8th August 1945, that is to say immediately after the destruction of Hiroshima, and before Nagasaki was effaced on the 9th, he sent a telegram to Truman in which he referred to the 'widespread anxiety as to whether the new power will be used to serve or to destroy civilisation', urging that Truman join him in making an immediate declaration that the UK and the USA were prepared to become 'trustees [of the atom bomb] for humanity in the interests of all peoples in order to promote peace and justice in the world'.[11]

When he succeeded to the Presidency on Roosevelt's death in April 1945, Truman was little wiser about nuclear matters than was Attlee. He had not been told about the existence of the Manhattan Project and, in the light of what has happened since, it is doubtful if he ever fully appreciated the nature and political significance of 'The Bomb'. All that Attlee effectively managed to get out of him, at a meeting in November 1945 in which the Canadian Prime Minister Mackenzie

King also took part, was a joint Declaration advocating the establishment of a United Nations Commission on Atomic Energy.[12] By that time Congress was already considering Senator McMahon's bill, which called for the strict American control of atomic energy. On 30th July 1946 the Atomic Energy Act, as it was called, was signed by Truman, and cooperation between the USA and Britain came to an end.

Following a recommendation of a small advisory committee which had been set up in September of 1945, Attlee had however already sanctioned the building of a nuclear pile to make fissionable material. Since there was no Labour Party Minister who was knowledgeable about the subject, Sir John Anderson, who had been in charge of nuclear affairs in Churchill's wartime coalition Cabinet, chaired the new Committee, which consisted of civil servants, scientists (among whom Sir James Chadwick was the most influential), and representatives of the Chiefs of Staff. This Committee had superseded a corresponding wartime body, the Tube Alloys Consultative Council, which had been set up by Churchill in 1941, also under Sir John's chairmanship. When Attlee set up the new committee, the Chiefs of Staff had been asked how many nuclear bombs they wanted. The answer was 'a stock to be measured in' hundreds, later stated to be 600—a number to all effects and purposes drawn out of a hat.

Despite their intimate knowledge of the nature and destructive power of atomic weapons, none of the physicists who sat on Anderson's new Advisory Committee appears to have appreciated fully what some of their

American opposite numbers had already seized upon, that the bomb would not only create a watershed in international relations, but that it was not a 'military' weapon in the sense that generals or air marshals or admirals could control the consequences of its use. They did, however, tell Anderson that the 'pile' which Attlee had sanctioned would need to be 'enlarged' if enough fissile material was to be produced for the bombs demanded by the Chiefs.

Anderson approached Attlee to get the further sanction, and the latter then arranged a meeting with the handful of his colleagues who were in the picture —Bevin, Cripps, Alexander, and Dalton. It took place in October of 1946. Michael Perrin, the administrative chief of the secret group that was dealing with the matter in the then Ministry of Supply, was also present. He records that Bevin arrived late on the scene but at a moment when, for reasons of cost, Attlee and his colleagues were about to decide against the building of a gaseous diffusion plant to enrich uranium. Bevin turned on his colleagues and said: 'We've got to have this . . . I don't mind for myself, but I don't want any other Foreign Secretary of this country to be talked at or to by the Secretary of State of the United States as I have just been in my discussions with Mr Byrnes. We've got to have this thing over here, whatever it costs.'[13]

The final decision to go ahead with the production of a British bomb was taken on 8th January 1947,[14] without any but a few knowing what had been brewing for over a year, and without any consideration of the repercussions that the decision would have on other spheres of national policy. As a major power, the UK had to have the bomb, not as a so-called 'deterrent'— that term was introduced later—but as a real weapon of war.

THE BOMB AND THE CHIEF SCIENTIFIC ADVISER

The three top scientists who were involved at this stage—Sir John Cockcroft, Sir James Chadwick and Sir Christopher (later Lord) Hinton—knew a great deal about nuclear physics and engineering, but nothing about the direction of war. The Chiefs of the three Services knew about war, but nothing about nuclear physics or how the bomb could be used in military operations. And to the best of my knowledge—and I was acquainted with all six and on close terms with one of them—not one, either scientist or military man, had really thought the matter through. But—and here comes the bizarre part of the story—that is what some other 'top' scientists had done. But their views went unheeded.

As I have said, the Government had set up an Advisory Council on Scientific Policy (the ACSP) to deal with matters relating to civil science and the supply of scientific manpower. Herbert Morrison was then the member of the Cabinet responsible for 'science', and before the ACSP was formed I had addressed to him a personal memorandum[15] in which I had argued that whatever central scientific advisory body was set up to help the Government, it should cover both defence and civil matters in which science played a part. My advice was rejected. Instead, a newly-formed Ministry of Defence set up a quite separate Defence Research Policy Committee (the DRPC) to decide the priorities for R&D expenditure on proposals for new weapons systems that came from the three Services, and to monitor the progress of those which were accepted. Sir Henry Tizard, one of the most experienced and worldly men of science in the country, was prevailed upon to become the Chairman of both the ACSP and the DRPC. In effect, he therefore became Chief Scientific Adviser to the Government as a whole.

The secret debate that was to lead to the decision that Britain should become an independent nuclear power was going on when these administrative committee matters were being settled. The outcome was all but a foregone conclusion. Hinton had already started designing a nuclear pile to produce plutonium. As I have said, he had been given authority to go ahead in late 1945. The decision was not, however, formally ratified until January of 1947, a few days after Tizard had taken up his dual appointment as Chairman of both the ACSP and the DRPC. Not until he had been six months in office—by which time very little progress had yet been made, either in the actual building of the pile or in much else—was he brought into the picture. He then let it be known that, in his considered opinion, the decision that Britain should become an independent nuclear power was unwise both from the political/strategic and the military points of view. So far as I know, his views were never formally debated by those who disagreed with him. Moreover, the issue was never discussed by the DRPC, even though this Committee in theory covered the whole spectrum of defence research.

The reason for his deliberate exclusion may in the first place have been a hangover from the well-known clash between Cherwell and Tizard that had started in the 1930s. Tizard—not Cherwell—had been an influential and critical figure in the secret and official scientific discussions that took place at the start of the war about the possibility that a nuclear bomb could be made. When Churchill became Prime Minister in 1940, it was Cherwell who had his ear, and in 1942 Tizard decided to leave Whitehall for Oxford. Once Cherwell knew that the bomb could work (he was sceptical about the possibility at the start), he was all for it—and even though no longer in office, he was in a position to press his views on John Anderson, with whom he had served in Churchill's wartime Government.

After his move to Oxford, Tizard had, however, continued to exercise some influence on the 'top' scientists who were directly engaged in military affairs, and early in 1945 the Chiefs of Staff had suggested to Churchill that Tizard should chair a Joint Technical Warfare Committee to advise on post-war defence. Anderson, as Chairman of the Consultative Council on nuclear matters, accordingly proposed to Churchill that Tizard, together with the Chiefs of Staff, should be fully informed about the nuclear secret. Churchill agreed about the Chiefs, who until then had been kept in the dark, but advised that Tizard 'should not be made a party at the present time'.[16] Not surprisingly, this instruction did not please Tizard (who presumably had been told by the Chiefs what they wanted), and he made his objections clear to General Ismay, the Prime Minister's intermediary with the Chiefs. When Ismay told Churchill how Tizard felt, he was instructed to re-read the minute Churchill had already written on the subject, 'and reply [to Sir Henry] in that sense on my behalf. . . . He surely has lots of things to get on with without plunging into this exceptionally secret matter. It may well be that in a few years or even months this secret can no longer be kept. One must always realise that for every one of these scientists who is informed there is a little group around him who also hear the news.'[17]

What can be regarded as the most important decision on a scientific and technical matter that was taken by government in the years since the Second World War, a decision with immense and continuing political and economic repercussions, was thus taken without reference to the Government's Chief Scientific Adviser, and without any real debate by the body—the DRPC—that had been set up to decide R&D priorities over the whole field of Defence.* Our generals, admirals and air marshals then had no more idea than did their

---

* From 1960 to 1971, when I was, first, Chief Scientific Adviser to the Minister of Defence, and then to the Government as a whole, the DRPC, over which I presided for some four years, never had nuclear matters on its agenda. At the technical level the subject was dealt with separately within a small nuclear enclave, over which I also presided. According to the evidence given in 1981 to the Lords' Select Committee by Sir Ronald Mason,[18] then the Chief Scientific Adviser to the Ministry of Defence, that is still the way it is.

opposite numbers in the USA or the USSR how the new weapon would affect tactics or strategy. As Kenneth Harris, Attlee's biographer, relates, all that mattered, so far as Attlee was concerned, was that America might retreat into isolationism, with Britain left on its own to resist Russian expansion to the west. 'Britain could not have resisted the Russian advance with conventional weapons. It is therefore not surprising that the chiefs of staff asked for the British bomb. A prime minister would have taken a great risk if he had decided to refuse their request. Attlee had no doubts about it.' In his own words, 'If we had decided not to have it, we would have put ourselves entirely in the hands of the Americans. That would have been a risk a British government should not take. It's all very well to look back, and to say otherwise, but at that time nobody could be sure that the Americans would not revert to isolationism—many Americans wanted that, many Americans feared it. There was no NATO then. For a power of our size and with our responsibilities to turn its back on the Bomb did not make sense.'[19]

For scientists now in the upper reaches of the bureaucracy, the lesson of the story is plain. Even when the advice which they might tender derives from un-rivalled knowledge, it does not follow that it will be heeded.

THE ACSP AND THE DRPC

As the only survivor of the Barlow Committee, and as Deputy-Chairman of the ACSP from the second year of its existence until it was wound up in 1964, I find it interesting to recall that Chadwick, who was convinced that we had to have the bomb, and who I believe knew more than any other scientist about the decisions on policy that were being taken,* became one of the first members of the ACSP. He was also Chairman of an ACSP sub-committee on nuclear energy which, ostensibly, was set up to deal only with its civil applications. Cockcroft, who succeeded Chadwick as its Chairman, was the only other member of the ACSP who served on this sub-committee. I was in the chair of the ACSP on the single occasion when the sub-committee reported to its parent body. The matter of our becoming an independent nuclear power was never discussed.

Chadwick, again, while a member of the ACSP, and the man who was most closely associated with the American nuclear weapons programme, was never a member of the DRPC, and Patrick Blackett, who had been a member of the Barlow Committee, was not invited to be a member of either body, although he had been appointed by Attlee to the Advisory Committee on Atomic Energy, which he had set up under Anderson. The omission of Blackett's name from the ACSP and DRPC was not surprising, since he had taken it upon himself to advise Attlee, and advise him forcibly, against the course the Government was about to pursue. In November of 1945, he had circulated a paper[20] to

---

* At the time he was also closer than any other British scientist to General Groves, the Director of the American Manhattan Project.

the Prime Minister and to his colleagues, in which he spelt out views which he later elaborated in his book, *The Military and Political Consequences of Atomic Energy*, which was published in 1948.[21] Blackett could see a nuclear arms-race developing, with no one the better off for it. And if America tried to bomb Russia out of existence with atom bombs (Russia had none at the time), the probable outcome 'would be to destroy much of the Soviet homeland, but also to extend Soviet power over nearly the whole of the European mainland, much of the Near and possibly also the Far East'.[22] Blackett's advice was that failing a comprehensive agreement on arms control and non-aggression, Britain should as soon as possible announce that for a period of up to ten years she had no intention of manufacturing atomic weapons, nor of acquiring any from the USA. He also advised that the UK should approach the young United Nations with the offer to open any of our nuclear plants to unilateral inspection and international control.

A man so outspoken in his opposition to government policy could hardly have become a member of the ACSP, and after 1947, Blackett took no further part in any official discussions relating to the bomb. It would have been remarkable if he had been accepted as a colleague by Marshal of the RAF Lord Portal, who had been appointed the administrative chief of Britain's nuclear effort. Blackett had been highly critical about RAF Bomber Command's wartime offensives, and had little respect for Portal's judgment.

If Attlee paid scant, if any, attention to the views on nuclear matters advanced by Tizard, officially his

Chief Scientific Adviser, or to those of Blackett, who was seemingly a political ally, it would appear that the affairs of the two scientific advisory bodies which he himself had set up also made little impact on him. They are not referred to either in the 'life' which he himself wrote,[23] or in Kenneth Harris's far more extensive biography.[24] The matters that came before the two Councils clearly were of little or no political interest to the Prime Minister. It is worth noting, too, that both the ACSP and DRPC survived through the 1950s and into the 1960s, when Harold Wilson took office, and that it is a measure of the political insignificance of the issues which both bodies debated that neither Council is referred to in the memoirs of either Harold Macmillan or Harold Wilson. As it turned out, the DRPC simply became a forum where mundane matters regarding defence R&D were secretly settled, or supposedly settled, while the ACSP dealt mainly with issues which, however important to the scientific community, were not critical to government.

Some twenty years ago I gave my view of the achievements of the ACSP, in a paragraph which I contributed to the final annual report of the Council. As I saw it, the ACSP was never inhibited 'when it discussed problems in which no other body had a particular vested interest—for example, questions such as the growth and deployment of scientific manpower, the scale of financial support for basic research, and matters concerning certain aspects of our overseas scientific relations. But throughout its existence it not surprisingly found itself impotent, and often baulked, when it came to advising either about the use of scientific and technological resources in executive departments of state, for example, the Defence Departments, or about the programmes of the research councils.'[25]

The observation that scientists should be on tap, not on top, is usually attributed to Winston Churchill. With extremely few exceptions, such as Lord Cherwell, that is how it has always been. During the twelve years that I served as a full-time civil servant, whenever necessary I tendered my advice directly to the Ministers I served or to the Prime Minister. But I also kept in the closest possible touch with my civil service colleagues, from whom I always had much to learn, particularly when my views on matters of policy differed from theirs. One of my permanent secretary colleagues once rebuked me because he had heard repeated a light-hearted remark I had made at a dinner party, to the effect that although Chief Scientific Adviser to the Government, the day I learnt that a piece of my advice had been acted upon, I would know that it was bad advice.

Lone voices in the world of Whitehall, whether those of scientists or of humanists in the administrative class, never have much chance of being heeded when they oppose some piece of conventional wisdom that has become institutionalised over the years. In 1946 Attlee might have banned the bomb. But today? What government, what prime minister, could handle the political consequences on the international stage of an outright ban? The problem for the scientist is to provide sensible and reasoned advice at the start, and to fight for its acceptance. That is the time and place for dispassionate advice—I will deal with the meaning of 'dispassionate' in a moment. When I began my stint as a paid public servant I was asked to call on Mr Macmillan (now the Earl of Stockton), the Prime Minister. He wanted me to pay close attention to the cost of Defence R&D. 'If it should be killed, kill a project when it's a minnow', he advised. 'It's more difficult when the minnows are as large as sprats, and all but impossible when they're the size of herrings.'

VESTED TECHNICAL INTEREST

'Pet projects' are, of course, only to be expected in establishments whose business it is to encourage particular fields of development. This is why technical and scientific advice to government is so often tinged by some vested interest which is not easily uncovered in an environment of bureaucratic secrecy. The situation is far better in the United States, where the system of congressional enquiry makes it normal for scientists in government employ to have to defend positions they have taken before what, in effect, is a jury of informed but independent scientists. The working of this system is well illustrated by the story of the anti-ballistic missile (ABM) system which was so powerfully urged by scientists and engineers in government employ, and equally powerfully opposed by most independent scientists who testified to congressional committees. While recognising that the system could not work, President Johnson had to continue the American programme, his reason being that the research and engineering effort to devise

a defensive system had been going on for so long—
indeed, it had been in progress for every bit of ten
years—and at so enormous a cost, that cancellation
would lay him, a Democratic President, open to the
charge by the Republican opposition that he was
responsible for 'an ABM gap'. In the event it was a
Republican President, Nixon, who in the SALT I
agreement, ended the dream that a politically meaningful defence against nuclear ballistic missiles could
ever be devised. Presumably Kosygin, who was party to
the agreement, was of the same mind.

Professor George Rathjens of MIT, a man who
has spent many years working for the Federal Government in Washington, has analysed the background of
the individuals who took part in the ABM technical
debate. It turns out that the great majority of those who
argued that ABM defences were a practicality, obtained
their 'research support' from the Pentagon, while most
of those who were 'against' were, in this respect, innocent. The President's Science Advisory Committee
was 'almost unanimous in its opposition'. Rathjens also
observes that the technical experts sent by the Pentagon
to persuade the Congressional Committees proved totally unable to substantiate their claims in the face
of the criticisms levelled by experts *not* in the Administration's service, and who were also called to give
evidence. This, as Rathjens notes, demonstrates 'the
difficulty of getting technical advice on matters of public policy that is *both* disinterested and informed'. [26]

Scientists in the British bureaucracy operate in far
more closed communities than do their opposite num-

bers on the other side of the Atlantic. One reason is that there is little mobility within the Scientific Civil Service. A second is that scientists and engineers in British universities are, in general, less interested in what goes on in government than are their American colleagues. A third is the difference between the British and American systems of government.

SCIENTIFIC AWARENESS

Much has been said over the years about the need to recruit more scientifically trained people into the administrative class of the Civil Service. Clearly this would be a good thing, as would, *ipso facto*, raising the scientific awareness of the population as a whole. We also hear today about the desirability of encouraging people in the public service to become what has been styled 'technological generalists'. Sir Hermann Bondi has added his voice to the many which have expressed regret that the top levels of the Civil Service are 'unable to recruit sufficient numbers of people . . . who have a sympathy for, and an interest in, science'.[27]

I myself am sceptical about the widespread belief that the majority of recruits now entering public service have little understanding of the scientific or technological considerations that affect so many aspects of government policy. Nor can I recall any senior civil servants who, as it were, shut their ears to whatever arguments of a technical or scientific kind that I may have wished to introduce into discussions of policy. They may have been hostile to the conclusions, but they certainly listened to the argument. It is surely not the lack of scientific knowledge that is the problem. Some scientists are more ignorant of the work of others than would be a well-read layman. I am sure that I learned far more from my classically-trained colleagues about the need to bring precision into the consideration of public affairs than I ever did from the majority of my scientific colleagues, some of whom, because of their technical obsessions, knew only how to deploy arguments to reach conclusions which suited their vested interests.

Obviously, it would be a good thing if at least a proportion of our top administrators had enjoyed a general scientific education. No doubt, too, the 'administrative class' would benefit from an admixture of 'technological generalists'. But what matters most at the levels where decisions on major policy are taken is not agreement about scientific theories or experimental observations. As I have said, what matters is the time when the scientific input is made, and it is the objectivity with which facts are deployed to the particular goal that is being discussed. Lack of familiarity with technical jargon, by those on whom the responsibility for decision rests, will always be a disadvantage when issues of policy that are affected by scientific and technological considerations are being discussed. Correspondingly, however, a scientific education, and still less a technological obsession, is not a sufficient condition for wise judgment. Can we lay the blame on the administrative class of the Civil Service—or indeed on ministers—for the enormous volume of resources that has been wasted on abandoned technological projects?

The answer is in general 'No'. Ministers and civil servants not only need dispassionate scientific advice, but maps of the hidden rocks of vested and prejudicial opinion. What is wanted is an increased awareness among higher civil servants and ministers that technical argument can be easily steered to predetermined conclusions.

We need to remember that the complaint that the voice of the scientist is not heard when major decisions are taken was not, and still is not, restricted to the field of government policy. In the early discussions of the ACSP we used to bemoan the fact that there were too few scientifically trained people—I am not differentiating here between scientists and engineers—on the boards of companies. Since then, there have been many, some of them chairmen of very large companies, and many who were and are highly distinguished in their basic professions. The country's fortunes have nonetheless continued to decline. Scientists in high places are not a sufficient condition for either industrial or national economic success.

SCIENTISTS IN HIGH PLACES

So what is it that we want from scientists in government? What do we expect from them? When scientifically qualified and experienced people become permanent or deputy secretaries—as some have—do we expect them to behave differently from those of their non-scientific colleagues at the top of the Civil Service? If we do, I fear that we are going to be disappointed. The daily schedule of either a permanent or a deputy secretary consists of much work and little science. What, too, do we want from advisory councils whose members are distinguished independent scientists? Have they a special role to play? And is there merit in appointing to the top scientific position in a government Department someone who up to the moment he sat down at his new desk knew nothing of the Department's affairs; someone who had probably never met one of the army of scientists he is now supposed to lead; and who perhaps had never spoken to a cabinet minister in his life; someone who may be not only innocent of party politics, but who before being recruited into government service may have evinced less concern about those issues of politics which transcend party differences than scholars educated in the humanities?

Let me begin to answer these questions by referring to chief scientists and chief scientific advisers in Departments. Their duties have remained basically unchanged throughout the post-war years. The men and women concerned have the routine responsibility of answering requests for technical information which relates, at almost every level of the bureaucratic hierarchy, to the enormous load of day-to-day work that goes on in their Departments. They have to anticipate the need for information, and to be clear about whatever research and/or development work may be required in dealing with particular problems. *

* This work may be done in departmental research establishments when they exist, or by the research councils, or by universities—and in the case of Departments such as Defence and Energy, in the R&D establishments of industry. Over the years, some research establishments which before operated under the umbrella of a research council

In some Departments managerial functions have been added over the past fifteen years to what previously may have been responsibilities which were essentially advisory. The reverse has also happened. Twenty years ago, when I was Chief Scientific Adviser in Defence, I was also notionally responsible for several establishments which now have been transferred to the Procurement Executive. Today the Chief Scientist in the Ministry of Defence has not only been relieved of these responsibilities, but he now reports to the Permanent Secretary and not to the Secretary of State.

As I have already tried to make clear, the degree to which departmental policies derive from, and depend upon, scientific considerations varies enormously, as does the extent and frequency with which policies need to be changed. In a department such as Agriculture there can never be disputes of substance about such matters as the eradication of animal disease, or about the advantages of one variety of wheat over another. Where disputes occur about, say, adverse public reaction to factory farming, or the opposition of conservationists to a proposal to drain land, the decisions that have to be taken are not scientific but political. Gov-

---

have been transferred to the Departments mainly concerned with their field of work. Thus the Building Research Station and Road Research Laboratory, which before the Second World War were part of the DSIR, are now controlled directly by the Department of the environment and the Ministry of Transport. Such changes in part reflect the regrouping that has taken place in Departments themselves, and doubtless there will be others in the future.

ernmental agricultural policies are updated only when new scientific knowledge emerges, and as economic and political circumstances dictate. On the other hand, in some areas of government, political expediency and economic considerations will necessarily qualify the use that is made of scientific developments. Thus, in Health, it is the availability of resources, not a lack of knowledge, which will in the end determine how far the life-expectancy of sufferers from certain diseases can be extended by health care. The Energy scene is different again. In the post-war period it has been upturned time and time again through the interaction of technical, political and economic factors. The downturn in economic activity has affected demand, the exploitation of oil and gas has conflicted with the interests of the coal industry, and the development of nuclear power has created endless problems. Other departments have also undergone revolutionary changes due to new technical knowledge. The old Post Office, now separated into British Telecom and the Post Office, maintained a powerful R&D Department from which a host of remarkable technical developments emerged, but only a fraction of which, mainly for lack of investment resources, have ever been made use of, a situation which seemed to be accepted by the people concerned more with cynical resignation than with despair.

The Ministry of Defence is clearly a case on its own. The Department is responsible for somewhat more than half of the Government's total expenditure on R&D; in 1986 the net cost of R&D to the Defence Budget was some £2,500 million. Most of the scientists and engineers in the many Defence R&D establishments were recruited straight from their universities, and have devoted, or will in due course spend, the greater part of their working lives in one narrow field of enquiry, using new scientific knowledge to improve old equipment or to devise new—and, to the extent that discourse is allowed, exchanging ideas only within the closed community in which they work. Except in the short term, so-called 'operational requirements' are always formulated around technological promises which, as often as not, turn out to have been over-ambitious. Defence scientists are at the heart of a very competitive business, and it is hypocrisy to deny, as some do, the basic proposition that defence R&D is at the heart of the arms-race. They are also involved in a trade in which the arms-producing countries buy from each other, cooperate with each other, and fight each other for the markets in which they sell their costly wares.

It is where the technical 'unknowns' dominate a proposed and costly new development, and where judgment about alternatives has to be exercised, that Chief Scientific Advisers in Defence face their real test. If they are to contribute meaningfully to decisions on policy, they must operate as equals with their equivalent service and civil service colleagues. They have to analyse problems not only in technical but also in strategic terms. A Chief Scientific Adviser in Defence cannot afford to subcontract his judgment, or bend it to fit a body of confirmed opinion. As a scientist he has to challenge accepted wisdom. The engineer at the bench asks whether he can reduce the weight of the aero-engine without at the same time reducing the speed and endurance of the aircraft it powers. The scientist at the top has to ask what it is all in aid of: can we defend ourselves better if we do this rather than that? And if a chief scientific adviser—or indeed any adviser—in a Department finds himself at odds with departmental policy, it is his duty to see that his views are known.

SCIENTIFIC ADVICE AT THE CENTRE

Only in theory would it be possible to formulate a 'National Science Policy Statement' in which were indicated those fields of basic science which it would be most useful to explore, and those which were ripest for economic exploitation. As things are, each Department separately includes in its supply estimates, a figure to cover its R&D programme, and then negotiates the whole bill with the Treasury. Only if he were very well-informed and personally curious would the Chief Scientific Adviser of one Department question a colleague's R&D budget. It would be a miracle were he to decide that some items in his own programme should be sacrificed in the national interest in order to release R&D resources which his colleague could use. In its reply to the Lords' Committee Report, the Government admitted that it has not up to now tried to make a horizontal survey of all departmental R&D projects in order to compare their relative costs and benefits. But a direct comparison would be meaningless. The 'benefit' of work on, say, some new form of heat exchanger cannot be compared with that of an enquiry into a new variety of wheat. Nonetheless, it is encouraging that the Chief Scientist in the Cabinet Office has now been charged to make an 'across-the-board survey' of governmental R&D. He is in a better position to do the job than is any departmental CSA, or any administrative under-secretary.

But there is a snag. The justification for any R&D carried out by a Government Department is that it is needed for the discharge of the Department's statutory responsibilities. If an across-the-board survey were to reveal some doubtful item, a central authority should, of course, challenge a Department to prove that the principle of departmental necessity had not been disregarded. But only a senior Cabinet Minister, or someone acting with the full authority of the Prime Minister, could have a project upturned against the wishes of the departmental minister. Moreover, resources for R&D that were in the estimates of one Department would, if released, not necessarily be transferred to another. It will therefore be interesting to see what lessons can be learnt from the exercise that is now being carried out, apart from its value in making departmental chief scientists aware of one another's problems.

There are, of course, a number of other tasks which are appropriate to a scientific office at the centre of government. First, a 'scientific centre' should continue the work that has been so well launched by the Advisory Council for Applied Research and Development (ACARD) in gathering and disseminating information about promising fields of technological exploitation.

Government needs no advice from scientists about the help it might proffer to dying industries, but advice can be valuable in indicating which new industries it would be wise to encourage. If, however, what is done is to bear the fruit that it should, it has to be done on the right scale, at the right time, and in the right way. There is little point in the government taking hesitant steps to enter an industrial market that is already dominated by overseas competitors who, to keep ahead, can spend far more than we can.

The 'centre' should also be responsible to the Prime Minister and Cabinet for organising special enquiries into the merits of costly but debatable technological ventures that might be promoted by Departments. And, in my view, it should also have the responsibility of coordinating advice about health and safety regulations and about environmental matters—advice which now flows in from so many quarters. This is an issue of such wide import, and one which is so sensitive politically, that it far transcends the interests of only a few Departments. It should, for example, be the responsibility of the 'scientific centre' to review all the evidence on matters such as the deleterious effects of lead in the environment, and to provide the best 'objective' advice about necessary action, taking into account both industrial and other implications. Finally, the 'centre' should continue to deal with those of our international scientific relations as stem from the treaty organisations to which we belong, and several of which now concern environmental matters, at the same time as it coordinates information about the adequacy of the resources which the Exchequer provides for basic science, not only to sustain the applied science of today, but also to assure the growth of the knowledge out of which the innovations of tomorrow will flow.'

THE HUMAN FACTOR

In his Reith Lectures, Sir Douglas Wass described the close personal relationship that normally develops between ministers and their permanent secretaries. 'A minister's job is a lonely one and his colleagues are not always his close friends and confidants. . . . By contrast, a senior official has no political ambitions and has a deep personal commitment to the success of his chief. They spend a lot of time together and share intimate thoughts. If the official's judgment is respected he comes to play a bigger part in policy formulation than any of the minister's political colleagues.'[28]

How about the relation of scientific advisers to ministers—and indeed, to permanent secretaries? In his day, Tizard was the 'scientific centre'. One reason why he was unable to make his voice heard on the nuclear issue—whether his view was right or wrong is now neither here nor there—was that, whereas he was on the best of terms with service chiefs and top civil servants, he had no link of friendship either with Attlee or with any other senior ministers. Another difficulty was the intense secrecy with which Attlee, following Churchill, enveloped the subject. Unless one was a member of the magic atomic circle, one could not have known that it existed. Today it is common knowledge

that such a circle does exist. Some years ago, when I
was Chief Scientific Adviser to the Government, a Cabinet Minister, not one 'in the inner ring', invited me
to lunch in an effort to winkle out some of the circle's
secrets. I had immediately to say that, even though it
was a Cabinet Minister and Privy Councillor who was
seeking information, I was not at liberty to disclose
anything, but that if instructed by the Prime Minister,
I would do so. I enjoyed my lunch, but heard no more
about the matter. If a request ever was made to the PM
it was obviously not approved.

While it never occurred to me then to question
the way in which our nuclear decisions are taken, I
have recently come to the view that the dense veil of
secrecy that shrouds British nuclear affairs—and other
technical affairs too—and which, for all we know, may
be penetrable by our potential enemies and competitors, can be prejudicial to our national interest. Obviously we do not want to risk revealing technical secrets
to any potential enemy. But discussion of highly important technical matters with strategic and economic
overtones within a small circle that not only has a vested
interest in the subject, but which is also shielded politically from informed and critical debate, does not
necessarily result in advice that leads to the wisest
political decisions.

I do not wish to touch here the very wide question
of 'open government'. Nor can I see the equivalent of
the American system of enquiry by Congressional Committees fitting into the British parliamentary system.
But while acknowledging the value of the work it is

already doing, I do see merit in considering whether the 'scientific centre' could be made an even more effective body than it is otherwise likely to become, by making it the servicing body for a central scientific and technological consultative council to consist of, say, twelve to fifteen scientists of independent judgment but with wide interests. Each of its members would serve a term of, say, no more than four years, and in this way there would be built up a reservoir of men and women of science with an interest in, and experience of, the affairs of government which transcend narrow departmental concerns. Such a body, with power to appoint *ad hoc* sub-committees, could, for example, have been charged to review all the evidence on the ABM issue that had already been made public in the United States—and very little of which had appeared in the British press—before the Chevaline programme to modify the warheads of our Polaris missiles was officially endorsed. They could have taken evidence in secret; they could have cross-examined our own defence scientists who wanted to make costly changes in the warheads, and even had them argue, in the presence of American 'experts', the strategic case for trying to adapt a warhead to deal with a single Russian target. That way, which unfortunately was not possible at the time, might have provided a clearer picture about the project than what was presented to the relevant ministers before decisions were taken. It would not, of course, be the concern of a central council of scientists to express views on such purely political matters as whether, for example, recourse to arms should be the policy in settling disputes, or whether controversies about fishing rights in our waters should be settled by a display of force. Nor would it be their business to consider any part of our treaty obligations other than derivative issues with scientific or technological repercussions, for example, regulations regarding food safety or the pollution of the environment. Equally, a central scientific council's concern with domestic policy should be confined to the preparation of advice about such technical matters as nuclear safety, or the merit of undertaking, and the likelihood of success of, costly technological programmes such as Concorde. In the latter case, again, it is worth remembering that, after very detailed and public technical debate, the vastly richer United States decided not to proceed with the development of its own supersonic carrier, whereas our Government, after secret and much more limited discussion, decided, in cooperation with the French, to go ahead.

It would be a sorry situation, indeed, were it now argued that, for reasons of security, matters of the kind to which I have referred could not be entrusted for discussion to a carefully selected body of our best and most open-minded scientists and technologists. We have lost grievously because many costly and finally abandoned projects had been left in the secret hands of even smaller technical groups with a vested interest in the outcome. We could hardly do worse than continue as at present.

It would take time to find the most effective individuals to constitute a central council. I am doubtful about the Lords' Select Committee recommendation that the membership of a central council should be in part representative of scientific and engineering institutions. That would make it too large and, in my view, unwieldy. We do not want a representative body when what is needed is informed advice. What is wanted is a small body of individuals who are not so much concerned with the promotion of science and technology as with those problems of government which are conditioned by scientific judgment. It has to be a body which, however difficult the task, can be relied upon to give dispassionate advice. Moreover, I believe it to be wrong to continue the process of disbanding one central scientific and technological committee only to replace it with another. ACARD now exists. If its membership is not adequate to achieve what is needed to discharge the wide range of responsibilities which I have defined, and which is more extensive than those encompassed by the new terms of reference it has recently been given, let ACARD change gradually as members complete the terms of their present appointment. And let those who replace them be individuals whose names command respect without their having to be the elders of science. We need men and women with open minds, not the leaders of fashion in specialised areas of scientific enquiry. We need youth and enthusiasm as well as experience. And since it is inconceivable that twelve, or fifteen, just men could be found without some of them entertaining a political prejudice one way or the other, let the rule be that as governments change, all members offer their resignations of which, however, no more than a third should be accepted. Four or five new appointments should be enough to adjust for any deviations of the council from the strict path of political objectivity.

In the years following the war, when Departments were encouraged to appoint scientific staffs, it was usual to recruit to the office of Chief Scientist or Chief Scientific Adviser men from outside the Scientific Civil Service. In those days, the men who were selected had, without exception, carried considerable responsibilities during the war years. That generation is now gone. Sir John Hoskyns declares that there is no staff college for would-be ministers. What I am suggesting here is one way of providing a school where scientists of distinction have an opportunity of learning about governmental administration and the world of politics, and of influencing decisions on policy which will shape the nation's future.

REFERENCES

1. Wass, Sir Douglas, 1984, *Government and the Governed* (1983 Reith Lectures), London: Routledge.
2. Hoskyns, Sir John, 1982, *Whitehall and Westminster: An Outsider's View*, London: Institute of Fiscal Studies.
3. *Report of the Committee on the Civil Service*, 1966–68 (Fulton Report) (Cmnd. 3638), London: HMSO, 1968.
4. Select Committee on Science and Technology, 1981, *Science and Technology I–Report*, London: HMSO.
5. Council for Science and Technology, 1982, *Technology and Government*.
6. Beveridge, W., 1942, *A Report on Social Insurance and Allied Matters*, London: HMSO (Cmnd 6404).
7. Powell, J. Enoch, 1966, *A New Look at Medicine and Politics*, London: Pitman Medical.

8. *Scientfic Manpower* (Barlow Report) (Cmnd 6824), London: HMSO, 1946.

9. *Higher Education* (Robbins Report) (Cmnd 2154), London: HMSO, 1963.

10. Gannicott, K. G., and M. Blaug, 1969, 'Manpower forecasting since Robbins,' in *Cornmarket Higher Education Review* (Autumn issue), and *Higher Education* (Robbins Report), *Evidence*, Part One, Vol. B, pp. 431, 433, London: HMSO, 1963.

11. Harris, K., 1982, *Attlee*, London: Weidenfeld and Nicolson.

12. Washington Declaration, 15 November 1945. *Appendix 4* in Gowing, M. and L. Arnold, 1974, *Independence and Deterrence*, 1, London: Macmillan.

13. Perrin, Sir Michael, in *The Listener*, 7 October 1982.

14. Clark, R. W., 1980, *The Greatest Power on Earth*, London: Sidgwick & Jackson.

15. Memorandum on the need for a central Government Science Secretariat, submitted by S. Zuckerman to Herbert Morrison, Lord President of the Council, on 16 September 1945.

16. Churchill to Anderson, 21 January 1945, in Clark (ref. 14).

17. Churchill to Ismay, 19 April 1945, in Clark (ref. 14).

18. Select Committee on Science and Technology, 1981, *Science and Government, II–Evidence*, London: HMSO.

19. See note 11.

20. Blackett, P. M. S., 1974, *Atomic Energy: An Immediate Policy for Great Britain*, *Appendix 8*, in Gowing, M., and L. Arnold, 1974, *Independence and Deterrence*, 1, London: Macmillan.

21. Blackett, P. M. S., 1948, *The Military and Political Consequences of Atomic Energy*, London: Turnstile Press.

22. See note 11.

23. Attlee, C. R., 1954, *As It Happened*, London: Odhams.

24. See note 11.

25. Zuckerman, S., 1970, *Beyond the Ivory Tower*, London: Weidenfeld & Nicolson.

26. Rathjens, G. W., 1982, 'The Scientific Community and Nuclear Arms Issues', in the Proceedings of the Symposium, *The Role of the Academy in Addressing the Issues of Nuclear War*, Washington, D.C.: American Council on Education, pp. 77–86.

27. Bondi, Sir Hermann, 'Science Graduates in Government', Letter to *The Times*, 18 June 1982.

28. See note 1.

9

Scientific Advice

Pronouncements about the part that science should play in governmental affairs and, correspondingly, about the social responsibility of scientists, have multiplied fast in recent years. Some have come from men who have wrestled in a practical way with the problem; others are the reflections of scholars who have surveyed the scene mainly from the sidelines. The Godkin Lectures on 'Science and Government', which C. P. Snow[1] delivered at Harvard in 1960, are among the better-known dissertations on the subject. The small volume in which they were recorded appeared hard on the heels of a celebrated essay in which Snow[2] had expounded his thesis of the two cultures—of the divide that separates followers of what he called a scientific culture, a culture characterised by 'common attitudes, common standards and patterns of behaviour, common approaches and assumptions', from those who adhere to the more traditional culture of the arts and humanities, and which, Snow then believed, was characterised by an 'unscientific flavour' that was in danger of turning anti-scientific.

The particular message which he tried to put across in the Godkin Lectures was that scientists should be 'active', not just at the top, but at all levels of government. The reason for his insistence on 'all levels' emerged from the dramatic account which he gave of the clashes about military policy that had occurred between two distinguished British scientists, Tizard and Cherwell, both of them 'top advisers' in the years before and during the Second World War. Because of his close personal relationship with Winston Churchill, Cherwell's advice prevailed, to the detriment, Snow argued, of the Allied cause in the war. A Postscript to the Lectures, which he published in 1962,[3] ended with the warning that it is dangerous to have a 'scientist in a position of isolated power, the only scientist among nonscientists . . . *whoever he is.*' 'Even a Vannevar Bush, in solitary power among nonscientists, carries a potential danger too heavy to be risked'—the risk being that he might exercise an unchecked and even irresponsible influence on political events. 'Whatever we do,' Snow urged, 'it must not happen again', 'it' meaning having one scientist in a position of particular power in the upper echelons of a hierarchy of politicians.

Yet, in spite of the widespread attention which Snow's plea aroused, this has happened repeatedly since the Second World War without the consequences that he feared materialising. There have been many scientific 'overlords', scientists at the top among men of power who have not been nurtured in a scientific culture. This, of course, is not to say that they were at the same time cut off from the rest of the scientific world. That they have never been. In America, the first full-time science adviser, James Killian, had been preceded by several part-time presidential advisers, including not only himself, but also, to mention a few others, Rabi, Piore, Bronk, and DuBridge. In addition, there have always been a multitude of scientific advisory bodies to governmental agencies, of which the most outstanding in the United States was certainly the President's Scientific Advisory Committee.

In the United Kingdom, too, we have had a vast network of scientific advisory committees to government, and also part-time science advisers to prime ministers. We have also had full-time chief scientific advisers in several government Departments, although it should be noted that none of these posts are political appointments in the sense that they are in the United States.

In recent years it has also become the fashion to try to formulate national science policies—whatever that term may be taken to comprehend. There have been international parliamentary and ministerial conferences on the subject. Only recently the United Nations convened a major international conference to consider the place of science and technology in the development of 'Third World' countries. From the sixties onwards, some governments have included ministerial portfolios to deal with science, occasionally, as in the case of Dr Pierre Aigrain in France, filled by men who are themselves working scientists. In the USSR several ministerial posts have always been filled by scientists and engineers. C. P. Snow, a distinguished novelist and at the same time a professional chemist, whose research interests had been in a field of physics, himself accepted a junior ministerial office in the Ministry of Technology which Harold Wilson set up when he became Britain's Prime Minister in 1964. Today one of the thirteen Commissioners of the Common Market includes in his portfolio responsibility for research and development. NATO too has an assistant director-general for scientific affairs.

Indeed, scientific overlords and overlords for science have multiplied since the war as fast as has the literature on national science policies. Snow foresaw clearly that there would be a reaction against the growing dominance of the scientific culture. Yet, as I have said, what he feared about the danger of having a chief scientific adviser at the top has not come to pass; at least no one has regarded it amiss that scientists have occupied positions of influence which at least on paper were the equivalent of that enjoyed by Cherwell during the war years. Equally, no one has suggested that the Western world has either become more secure, or the world as a whole more peaceful because there have been and still are scientific advisers 'at the top' in the company of political chiefs who have no direct experience of the scientific culture. Was there something wrong, therefore, with the conclusions that Snow drew from his story of the Tizard-Cherwell feud, or was the relationship of Cherwell to his political chief something *sui generis* from which no conclusions of a general kind could be drawn?

First, let me make the obvious point that the issue does not concern those scientifically and technically trained people who are government servants in every country where the State has become responsible for matters such as security, law and order, water supplies, and public health. In his authoritative work on the evolution of the relations between government and science in the United States, Don K. Price[4] pointed out that 'the development of government powers and functions' during the nineteenth century was 'only the inevitable adoption by politicians of ideas first developed in scientific laboratories and in scholarly or professional societies.' Obviously the Government would have been unable to discharge the responsibilities which it had assumed in this way without recourse to scientific advice. In 1963, Wiesner[5] reported that more than 60 per cent of all professional people then in the United States' civil service were trained scientists or technologists. Whatever the figure today, it is a revealing indication of the growth of governmental scientific institutions in the USA. From that point of view, it can be said that American scientists have certainly satisfied C. P. Snow's admonition that they should be active not just at the top but at all levels of government.

In European countries, where the State did not have to contend with problems deriving from the division of authority between Federal and State governments, the evolution of scientific and technical institutions to provide routine and regulatory advice to the central power did not follow precisely the same path as it did in the United States. For present purposes it will be sufficient to refer very briefly only to what happened in the United Kingdom. As I have said, the process began with the appointment by the Crown of a 'Master of the King's Ordnance' in 1414. But, as in all the emerging maritime countries, there was also a practical need to improve the techniques of navigation. This proved a powerful stimulus to the growth of astronomy and mathematics. In 1675, fifteen years after the Royal Society of London 'for Improving Natural Knowledge' had been founded, a Royal Observatory was set up as the first state-aided scientific institution. Then, after a gap of some 150 years, a Geological Survey, today called the Institute of Geological Sciences, was launched, not only to promote geological science in general but as 'a work of great utility bearing on mining, road making, the formation of canals and railroads, and other branches of national industry.' The office of Government Chemist followed in 1842. This was set up by the Department of Customs and Excise, and its first remit was to enquire into the adulteration of tobacco. Following the passage in 1875 of the first effective Food Act to be promulgated in any country, the responsibilities of the British Government Chemist were widened to deal with the harmful adulteration of food and, still later, with other related problems.

Despite these developments, the scientific concerns of successive United Kingdom governments during the nineteenth century were anything but urgent. Correspondingly, organised science in the shape of the Royal Society displayed little, if any, interest in affairs of state. But there were exceptions. From about the middle of the nineteenth century a few public figures, including Prince Albert, Queen Victoria's consort; T. H. Huxley, the zoologist; and Lyon Playfair, a professor of chemistry and the first scientist to become a member of any British government, kept sounding the message that Britain would decline in influence relative to Germany and France were steps not taken both to stimulate scientific education and to make industry more science-based than it was. In 1870 this led to a well-backed proposal for the appointment of a minister of science. Soon after, the 'immediate' creation of a ministry of science and education was advocated by a Royal Commission. If many of the recommendations of this illustrious body were politely brushed aside (in the case of the proposal for a minister of science, the translation of the word 'immediate' into action took all but a hundred years), they did at least stimulate the establishment in 1900 of a National Physical Laboratory and, in 1909, of a Development Commission to advise on scientific aid to agriculture, rural industries, and fisheries. Four years later, a Medical Research Committee, the forerunner of Britain's present Medical Research Council, was established. As part of the same wave of governmental interest, a Department of Scientific and Industrial Research was set up in 1916 and charged with the responsibility for putting forward proposals which could help trade and industry.

But there was still neither need nor place in the framework of British government for chief scientific advisers in the guise they are known today—that is to say, of *advisers who have to deal not only with the*

*furtherance of scientific knowledge and its applications,
but also with matters of national policy that are affected
by scientific considerations.* Indeed, the boot was on
the other foot. If politicians and scientists had in general
not yet recognised that science was a primary deter-
minant of social and political change, there were a few
political leaders who were greatly interested in science
as a part of culture. Arthur Balfour, Prime Minister
from 1902 to 1905, was esteemed highly enough as a
scholar not only to have been elected in 1888 a Fellow
of the Royal Society at the early age of 39, and President
of the British Association for the Advancement of Science during the period of his prime-ministership, but
to be sounded out to become President of the Royal
Society—an office which he declined. His uncle, Lord
Salisbury, who had preceded him as Conservative Prime
Minister on two occasions, was sufficiently interested
in science to set up his own private laboratory at Hat-
field, his great country house outside London.

The explicit recognition, or perhaps I should say,
the passive acceptance of the fact that government *qua*
government needs organised and continuing advice on
scientific matters because they are a critical factor in
social and economic change, started to surface in England only during the world war of 1914 to 1918. In
the four years that it lasted there were numbers of
major scientific and technical innovations—for example, aviation and chemical warfare—whose poten-
tialities and further development were well beyond the
comprehension of the military and political leaders of
the day. It was then that a few academic scientists emerged

as advisers and initiators of technical policies which affected the war effort. Some soon became prominent figures, among them A. V. Hill, G. I. Taylor, Harold Hartley, Tizard, and Cherwell.

When peace came in 1918 most of these wartime scientific advisers returned to their academic institutions. Only a very few continued to advise on military affairs, in particular as members of a sub-committee of the inter-war Committee of Imperial Defence, on which Tizard and Cherwell first clashed. There were, of course, many who became involved in the affairs of the government's medical, agricultural, and scientific and industrial research institutions, all of them bodies which encouraged basic as well as applied research. Behind the scenes there was always Tizard, who was looked to for scientific advice of a general kind, although he was certainly not the only channel through which scientific advice could flow to the Cabinet.

Then came the Second World War, during the course of which scientists and engineers in the UK and the USA were mobilised to further the national effort. As I have said, the central policy-making and coordinating body in the USA was the Office of Scientific Research and Development led by Vannevar Bush and Conant, with Lewis Weed directing the medical side. Related to it were many other wartime scientific and technological organisations, not least the Manhattan Project. The United Kingdom also had a considerable network of scientific organisations, but there was no powerful body at their head, possibly because Cherwell was always at Churchill's side. He certainly saw no need to lend authority to a newly-appointed body called the Scientific Advisory Committee to the Cabinet which, in effect, consisted only of the officers of the Royal Society and the heads of the Research Councils. But even if there was no single focal point at the top, British scientists and engineers, instead of remaining restricted to purely technical matters that related to the development of military equipment, started to busy themselves with the operational problems which the use of new technological devices demanded. They became middlemen, interpreters of science, and sometimes even men of action.

This was not surprising. Advanced and novel technological devices, for example radar units, could not just have been handed over to be operated either by conventional military personnel, however professional their service training, or to non-scientists who had left civilian jobs to become wartime soldiers. An understanding of the underlying science and engineering was essential. To fill the gap in the UK, some ten thousand university men with a scientific or engineering education were given special training and recruited into the armed services. Moreover, new weapons and weapon systems that had been developed at the frontiers of scientific and technological knowledge could not have been evaluated simply in theory. Those who had been involved in their design and development had to test them under operational conditions, not only to see what technical improvements were possible, but to make sure that the tactics of the operations that were designed in relation to the information provided by, for example, sonar or radar, were based on measurable fact. Basically, this is how operational research was born, beginning as a study of the way novel equipment worked in practice, and of the tactics that had to be developed to get the most out of new technical developments. Watson-Watt, the father of wartime radar, ponderously defined operational research, in whose formal evolution he had played a significant part, as 'the application of the basic scientific methods of measurement, classification, comparison and correlation to the selection of means for attaining, with the least expenditure in effort and in time, the maximum operational effect which could be extracted from the available or potentially available resources in personnel and material.'[6] A few British scientists became combat officers in order to test such new devices as air-borne radar. And there was Flight Sergeant J. M. Nissenthall, a technician, who took part in a commando raid whose object was the capture of an intact new German radar unit. A small number of operational researchers also became involved, not just with the interface between tactics and 'hardware', but with the design of actual operations. Separate military operations were in effect treated as experiments of a very crude kind. How closely did what was achieved correspond to what planners and commanders had set out to achieve? What lessons could be learnt that would be relevant to future plans? In my own case, this led to an intimate involvement in the now well-known dispute about the best strategic uses of the British and American heavy bomber forces.[7]

The idea of doing all this was indeed far from new.

There were certainly glimmerings in World War I of what later became formalised as operational research. And to go back even further, more than 200 years earlier Isaac Newton had written that 'If instead of sending the Observations of Seamen to able Mathematicians at Land, the Land would send able Mathematicians to Sea, it would signify much more to the improvement of Navigation and safety of Mens lives and estates on that element.'[8]

When hostilities ended in 1945, it came as no surprise that in the UK, no less than in the USA, political leaders, military chiefs and industrialists, who had seen scientists in action during the years of war wanted to involve them in the urgent problems of post-war reconstruction. Advice was increasingly needed to help make the best of the wartime and post-war scientific and industrial revolution. Moreover, there were many scientists who did not want to return to their university laboratories. Increasing amounts of public money were being invested in advanced technological industry, at first mainly in aerospace and the exploitation of nuclear power. There were new challenges and new opportunities everywhere. Military equipment was becoming ever more complicated as more and more new science was put to use. New navigational equipment based on inertial guidance systems was being developed. The nuclear, computer, and micro-electronic age had begun. A host of new drugs started to see the light of day. Then, in the sixties, governments found themselves having to deal with public concern about environmental pollution, about the exhaustion of resources, about population growth, about a whole variety of social and economic problems which seemed to stem from the ever-accelerating exploitation of new scientific knowledge. And scientists and engineers were everywhere in short supply.

With dramatic and seemingly endless social and economic changes stemming from the exploitation of new scientific knowledge, political leaders during this period found themselves faced with far more daunting problems than those with which politicians in any other period of human history had had to deal. In 1793, Coffinhal, the President of the French Revolutionary Tribunal, was able to dismiss Lavoisier's appeal against the death sentence with the words '*La République n'a pas besoin de savants.*'[9] Today the survival of advanced industrial societies is critically dependent on the *savants*. And with thousands of scientists and technologists within the structure of government, there have had to be scientific advisers at the top. In theory, if not in practice, how else could the work and influence of thousands of governmental scientists be coordinated, if indeed they can be coordinated?

There is, of course, another way of viewing the participation of the scientific world in the political changes of the past two to three decades. In stimulating change, in promoting the birth of new industries, in devising new agricultural techniques, and in encouraging the launching of vast new technological projects, scientists and engineers have not been acting simply as servants of politicians and military chiefs who could not themselves have known whether what was being considered was either technically possible or socially, economically, and politically desirable or necessary. Nor, as the years passed, were scientists simply called in to monitor new laws whose aim was to protect the ordinary citizen from being damaged by new hazards in the environment in which he lived and worked. The scientists and technologists were themselves the ones who initiated the new developments, who created the new demands, who warned the public about new hazards. They were the ones who, at base, were determining the social, economic, and political future of the world. Without any badge of authority conferred on them either by democratic decision or by autocratic diktat, without any coherent concern for political values or goals, scientists and engineers had become the begetters of new social demand and the architects of new economic and social situations, over which those who exercised political power then had to rule. The nuclear world, with all its hazards, is the scientists' creation; it is certainly not a world that came about in response to any external demand. So, at root, is the whole of today's environment of ever-rising material expectation. So, because of biomedical advances, is the spectre of overpopulation. So, some protest, is environmental pollution. So is the world of instant communications. So is the world of missiles. So is the unending arms-race by which we are all now threatened.

And here lies the real problem. Means have a habit of becoming ends, and scientists and technologists have not only been extending our understanding of the nature of the physical world; they have also been providing the means whereby the new physical and biological phenomena which they reveal can be harnessed in three-dimensional form for practical ends. The results of the exploitation of scientific and technological ideas are the aircraft and the refrigerators, the guns and the convenience foods, the nuclear power stations and the new drugs—all symbols of either national or consumer power in a competitive world. To an ever-increasing extent, major issues which are now at the heart of the deliberations of government have thus emerged—whether directly or indirectly is neither here nor there—as a result of the unplanned and unrestrained technological exploitation of new scientific knowledge.

Some now say that this is precisely what is wrong with the world; that if they are to discharge their social responsibilities, somehow or other scientists simply have to learn to appreciate what will be the wider consequences of new discovery. But no one supposes that scientists are furnished with crystal balls which reveal in advance the consequential social, economic, and political changes that derive from their enquiries. So, because the future cannot be mapped in advance, others now argue that knowledge is not an 'over-riding value'; that some kinds of enquiry into the unknown, some kinds of research, should be banned.

There is nothing new in this reaction. But the idea of controlling the advance of new knowledge has never been anything but an idle dream; and in my view it will always be an idle dream. No one can ban what is not yet discovered. It is impossible to put the unknown into chains. At every moment the future is at the mercy of some discovery not yet made. As Paul Valéry wrote: 'We move into the future backwards'—'*Nous entrons dans l'avenir à reculons.*'[10]

One could say that there is another reason why chief governmental scientific advisers are needed. Even if they cannot spell out the social and political consequences of major technological developments, their understanding of the scientific and technical facts can help make Valéry's backward journey less hazardous for political leaders than it might otherwise be. Obviously, therefore, scientific advisers shoulder great responsibilities. They may also, as Snow implied, exert great influence. But in the end their power is more apparent than real. Stanley Baldwin, Britain's Prime Minister at the time of the abdication of King Edward VIII, once referred to two newspaper barons as men who exercised 'power without responsibility—the prerogative of the harlot throughout the ages.'[11] It is the other way round with chief scientific advisers. My own view is that whatever their personal relationships with those who make up the upper echelons of a political hierarchy, and whatever responsibilities they shoulder, chief scientific advisers do not exercise the power which Snow had in mind. They might turn out to be good advisers, they might be bad advisers, but whatever they are, power, or its pretence, is squarely in the hands of those whom they advise, in the same way as history inevitably makes its judgments, not of advice, but of the action which flows from the decisions of political leaders.

In authoritarian regimes, the responsibility for final decision, and so for the outcome of the action that follows, is clearly that of the politicians at the top and of the ruling clique within which they operate. C. P. Snow cast Cherwell in the role of a bad adviser because of his advocacy of the bombing of German cities, a policy which he himself did not dream up, but which Snow supposed he might have overturned had he believed it to be wrong. Whether he would have succeeded, I am not so sure. My own example of a bad adviser would be Lysenko, whose advice prevailed with Stalin against that of every respected scientist in the USSR, with disastrous effects on Russian agriculture. Decades had to pass, Stalin had to die, before Lysenko was removed. Some sectors of Russian biology have not yet recovered from the results of his malign advice. But it was Stalin who was responsible for the influence which Lysenko wielded—not the other way round.

Is it any different in the Western world in which we live? Winston Churchill once said that 'No one pretends that democracy is perfect or all-wise. Indeed,' he went on, 'democracy is the worst form of Government except for all those other forms that have been tried from time to time.'[12] A cynical observation, some might say, but it is parliamentary democracy that nonetheless provides the framework within which the elected leaders of Western countries carry the responsibility for decision on the major technological issues that are now transforming the world—however limited or profound their knowledge and understanding may be of, for example, nuclear reactors or immunisation programmes or aero-engines or genetic engineering. Before deciding on any one of these matters, presidents or prime ministers might consult their scientific advisers or their political colleagues, or solicit or accept unsolicited advice. But once taken, the decision for action, whatever the level at which it is taken, whether it proves to be right or wrong, becomes the responsibility of the government in power, and above all of the man or woman by whom it is led. For that is the price that is paid by those who seek and achieve political power. In our kind of society only the electorate that has brought them to the top can inhibit presidents or prime ministers from acting either in accordance with, or against the counsels of the advisers, scientific or unscientific, on whom they may call, or against the multitude of political pressures by which they are beset.

The electoral systems whereby presidents and prime ministers come to power are, of course, not the same. Under the US Constitution a president serves a four-year term, and if re-elected can hold office for only one more. Given that he or she retains the leadership of the party to which they belong, and given that the party continues to be favoured by the electorate, the British system does not specify any limit to the period a politician can continue as prime minister. There are corresponding differences in the terms of service of top scientific advisers. As I have said, while the post of Chief Science Adviser to the President is, in effect, a political office, in the UK the corresponding position was treated as part of the permanent bureaucracy during the years that it existed—although there was nothing to stop the incumbent of the office from resigning should he so wish. That in fact is what my successor in the post did, with no reappointment being made after his departure, the formal reason being that since government Departments had greatly increased their scientific advisory strength in the preceding years, there was no particular need for a co-ordinating scientific office at the centre.

There is another difference between our two countries with respect to scientific advice at the higher levels of government. Over the years the United States has developed a much more effective and open exchange than prevails in the UK between university and industrial scientists on the one hand, and scientists in governmental agencies on the other. This is something we in the UK still have to develop. But whatever the institutional differences between our two countries, the problems faced by chief scientific advisers to heads of government are essentially the same.

When President Eisenhower warned the American public[13]—vainly as events have turned out—of the 'acquisition of unwarranted influence, whether sought or unsought, by the military-industrial complex' and of the 'danger that public policy could itself become the captive of a scientific-technological elite', his message was in fact directed to the peoples of all advanced industrial societies. What the President was proclaiming is the first major difficulty with which chief scientific advisers have to contend. The danger towards which he was pointing derives from the entire scientific-technological process, a process which no top scientific adviser, however wise and far-seeing, can command in the way an army commander can his troops. The field of scientific enquiry has become too vast, and its rate of growth, its rate of change, and the rate of potential application too rapid, for that ever to be possible. Even comprehensive surveillance by the best scientific staff one could assemble is extremely difficult—even in theory. The pure or fundamental science of today inexorably becomes the applied science and technology of tomorrow, with unforeseeable consequences, either immediate or remote, flowing from its exploitation.

The first fact that advisers at the top therefore have to accept is that most of the issues with which they deal will be controversial, and that their work will inevitably thrust them into the political arena. That is where sophisticated political as well as scientific judgment becomes essential. The second is that, whatever their personal relations with presidents or prime ministers, scientists at the top may be kept uninformed—on occasion perhaps even misinformed—by other scientific advisers and officials about what goes on in their separate and lesser domains in the vast machine of government. There is nothing surprising in this. For one thing, the sheer volume of scientific activity sets limits to possible consultation. For another, the enormous bureaucracies of today usually comprise separate empires, each with its own internal loyalties, and each concerned to further—or at least to protect—its own sphere of influence, regardless of its place within the framework of overall national policy. Central government is never perfect, and chief scientific advisers suffer as much as do their masters from its imperfections, and in the limitations of authority.

The third basic problem with which chief scientific advisers have to contend is that the methods of politics are not those of science. Politicians who wield power have to take account of all manner of sectional political pressures. Of necessity, they always have to be looking over their shoulders. This is as true of the United Kingdom, where the executive and legislative powers are in theory inseparable, as in the United States, where they are not. Moreover, room for manoeuvre enjoyed by presidents or prime ministers is inevitably constrained by the decisions of their predecessors, and by political pressures that derive from the action that has flowed from those decisions. Aneurin Bevan once remarked that when he takes office a new minister has only a day or so to decide and act for himself; if he fails to take advantage of his brief period of freedom he soon becomes the servant of his own servants. There was more than a grain of truth in the observation, however exaggerated the terms in which it was made.

There is a further difficulty. It is rarely possible for political decisions about national issues that are critically conditioned by scientific and technological considerations to be taken in isolation. Reservoirs—to cite a relatively trivial example—are not necessarily built in areas which are most suitable from the economic and technical points of view; governments may have to bend to pressure from local environmentalists and site them far more disadvantageously. And what government has not continued with vast defence projects, sometimes even with civil projects, when the best considered and most dispassionate advice from their chief scientific advisers has argued that the projects should be cancelled—that they were technological 'white elephants'?

While they usually have to operate in an environment of controversy, top scientific advisers can, however, expect to receive—and certainly have received—the full support of the scientific community when the influence they can bring to bear on government relates to the resources which should be devoted to scientific education and scientific research as a whole. This is where their role is essentially that of 'science advisers', of advisers who act on behalf of science generally, as distinct from that of scientific advisers whose concern is essentially with major matters of political concern that derive from, or are affected by scientific considerations. From this point of view, top advisers have also been very successful on the international stage. To cite one of many examples, it was through the efforts of those who served on the NATO Science Committee that the weaker members of the Alliance—and also many other countries—were first encouraged to devote adequate resources to scientific education and research. There is also the example of the establishment of such international organisations as CERN.

The scientific community can also be expected to be at one in its support of chief advisers in any general proclamation of the part that science should play in furthering developments in industry or agriculture or medical care or defence. But from here on difficulties arise. This is where the role of the adviser changes, where political judgment becomes critically important, where controversy enters.

The reason is simple. There is little, if indeed any, consensus in the community of scientists in areas of social and governmental policy which are affected by scientific considerations, or in matters which relate to technological exploitation. If one set of advisers declares that the world cannot do without nuclear power, another argues the reverse. If one urges the merits of water-cooled reactors, another campaigns for a gas-cooled variety. Scientists who deliver strident warnings about the dangers of chemicals used to preserve food are treated as alarmists by others. And so the debate rages, whether about nuclear power, or about the risks of cancer attendant on the use of some drug, or about overpopulation, or about the exhaustion of natural resources, or about environmental pollution.

Moreover, when it comes to the expression of opinion about the social or political implications of new technological developments, it is certainly not just a scientific élite—whatever meaning one attaches to the term—that has a voice. In a democracy, views about the benefits or disbenefits of applying a new piece of scientific knowledge or proceeding with some technological development can be expected from almost any quarter with a pretence to scientific knowledge. And such is the magic associated with the word 'science' that almost any message presumed to be scientific will usually make an impact on a section of a citizenry eager to accept whatever is disseminated in the name of science, and then to transform it into a focus of political pressure. 'Political conflicts', as Dr Nelkin[14] has put it, 'are basic realities of technological decisions'—a proposition which I would be inclined to qualify by saying 'of all *major* decisions'. From the moment that value judgments become the order of the day, scientific advisers at the top cannot but be embroiled in political argument.

There is no need to cite examples, but I am sure that it is nonetheless safe to say that political leaders— and here I refer not only to the UK and the USA, but to others as well—have on many occasions been able to rely with confidence on their top scientific advisers to steer them to wise decisions about costly technological projects. But at the same time, top advisers have proved unequal to the task of generating the informed consensus which is essential to political decisions that have to be taken in certain fields of technology. Perhaps the most prominent example of this today lies in the inability of chief advisers to achieve agreement in the scientific community about the best and safest policy for nuclear power. Nor is our record anything to be proud of in numbers of other cases where it is essential to reconcile safety and environmental concerns with the need to develop and assure both natural and industrial resources.

But above all, we have failed in what I hold to be—and I do not believe that I am alone in so doing —the most important single issue in which presidential and prime ministerial scientific advisers have been involved over the past forty years—the arms-race, and in particular the nuclear arms-race. It need not have happened, but it did.

For present purposes it can be said that the race started in 1946 with the refusal of the USSR to agree to the Lilienthal plan for placing all nuclear technology—military and civil—under UN control. Then in 1948 came the communist coup d'état in Czechoslovakia, followed by the blockade of Berlin and, in 1949, by the explosion of the first Russian atom bomb. The cold war had started. The NATO alliance of the Western powers was formed to counter the alliance of the Soviet bloc. Warnings that the Russians were well ahead of the USA in the size of their nuclear missile armoury—warnings of a so-called 'missile gap' which we now know did not exist—started to be fostered, and became a powerful political card in the run-up to the 1960 presidential election. A race into space was launched. Throughout this period both sides were testing nuclear warheads in the atmosphere, with the UK participating on its own, but to a lesser extent. Very soon there was worldwide concern about the serious health hazards associated with radioactive fall-out. Formal diplomatic and technical talks were started in Geneva to consider an international agreement to ban all tests.

In broad outline, this was the scene within which presidential science advisers, and to a lesser extent the top advisers in the UK, faced their most serious test. There are many published records of what happened, but I would refer here particularly to the writings of Killian,[15] President Eisenhower's first chief science adviser; to those of Kistiakowsky,[16] his second; of Wiesner, President Kennedy's adviser; and of York,[17] the first Director of Defense Research and Engineering in the Pentagon.

As I have said, the original idea had been a ban

on all nuclear tests, a ban which Harold Macmillan, President Eisenhower and then President Kennedy wanted. Mr Macmillan certainly believed that Khrushchev had the same goal in mind.

Unfortunately there was also acute opposition to any treaty. Regardless of the worldwide and, from the scientific point of view, thoroughly justified concern about fall-out, there were in fact many—including prominent scientists in the weapons laboratories of both our countries—who were opposed to any ban on atmospheric tests, leave alone an end to the elaboration of new warheads. Their 'hawkish' views carried considerable weight among the military, in Congressional committees, and in some sections of the public, who soon became persuaded that there was something to be gained by continuing the nuclear arms-race, and that anyhow the Russians would be bound to cheat, whatever treaty was agreed. *Ergo*, if there was to be a treaty, the Russians would have to submit to 'on-site' inspection. Since it soon became apparent that there was no chance that the Senate would ratify a treaty for a total ban on testing unless the Russians accepted this condition—which they made plain they would not do—President Kennedy then had to settle for one which did not preclude underground testing. As York wrote, 'one of the political prices' that the President had to pay in order to secure Congressional support for the Partial Test Ban Treaty of 1963 was a promise that the Atomic Energy Commission would embark on a programme of underground tests vigorous enough 'to satisfy all our military requirements'.

Because of the nature of the British parliamentary system, Mr Macmillan was in a position to overrule any opposition there might have been in the UK to a total ban—to which, in any event, there was none from any parliamentary quarter. But he, too, had to yield to the political pressures that were playing on President Kennedy. Regardless of the fact that the UK was a full even if a junior partner in the negotiations, and despite other considerations, the constraints which the legislature could impose on executive political power by virtue of the US Constitution affected the British Prime Minister as well as the President.

Today, when a comprehensive test ban has still to be negotiated, opposition to a possible treaty is once again coming from the same quarters as before, with the same old arguments—plus a few others—being deployed in an effort to hold up progress.

As I have said, the so-called missile gap turned out to have been a myth. Indeed, the Russians then started pressing hard to close the gap which *they* had perceived. This added another dimension to the arms-race, as did the dream of devising anti-ballistic missile systems. SALT I provided a check to the latter idea, but the size of the opposing nuclear arsenals nonetheless continued to increase. Today the declared purpose of SALT II is to establish a measure of nuclear equivalence between the two sides, but at a level which, were the present state of mutual deterrence ever to break down, would be well above the threshold needed to devastate utterly and without hope of repair, all the cities, even many of the small towns, of both the North

American and Eurasiatic continents, with hundreds of millions killed in a flash, and with most of those who were not so lucky then dying of the effects of radiation, of starvation, without medical or any other help. These are not extravagant statements. They are all spelt out in recent official American reports[18] which record the results of careful scientific analyses of what would happen at different levels of nuclear exchange. Similar conclusions were drawn from corresponding and even more detailed studies that were carried out in the United Kingdom about twenty years ago, and the general results of which were also published.[19] No one doubts that the Russians are as much aware as we are of these grim realities. Yet, however excessive the Western and Eastern nuclear arsenals might already seem, today it looks as though the price that will have to be paid for the ratification of the SALT II Treaty—given that it is ratified—might well be another vast increase of expenditure by both sides on so-called 'strategic systems' and on 'defence' generally.

What then were the chief science advisers doing as this scene unfolded? My answer would be that present prospects might well be worse than they are had the advisers not been there—we might not have had even a partial test ban. But in general we all failed. In 1964, a year after the Partial Test Ban Treaty was signed, York and Wiesner published an article[20] in which they stated that in assuring national security further tests of nuclear weapons were unnecessary. As they saw it, the increase in so-called military power which might follow from further testing and from the elaboration of more nuclear

weapons was bound, in both the East and the West,
to bring about a decrease in national security. In the
considered professional judgment of these two men—
and they had all the facts at their disposal—a continuation of the nuclear arms-race provided no escape
from this curious paradox. This conclusion, which York
later elaborated in his book *Race to Oblivion*,[21] is one
to which I had also in all logic been driven at the start
of my career as a chief scientific adviser. And York also
quotes a statement by Harold Brown, when Secretary
for Defense, to the effect that:

> Those who have served as civilian officials
> in the Department of Defense at the level
> of Presidential appointment . . . have rec-
> ognized the severely limited utility of military
> power, and the great risks in its use, as well
> as the sad necessity of its possession. . . . (The)
> higher their position and, hence, their re-
> sponsibility, the more they have come to
> the conclusion that we must seek national
> security through other than strictly military
> means . . . and urgently.

As long ago as 1957, a Government White Paper said
that there were then no means of protecting the British
population against the consequences of nuclear attack.[22] There are none today, when the scale of attack
that could be envisaged is at least a hundred times
greater than it was nearly thirty years ago. And, as I
argued[23] in the days when the Partial Test Ban Treaty

was being negotiated, neither is there any military reality to what is now referred to as theatre or tactical nuclear warfare, a field-war in which nuclear weapons are used. The logic which leads to that particular conclusion has never been controverted. There are no vast deserts in Europe, no endless open plains, on which to turn war-games in which nuclear weapons are used into a reality. The distances between villages are no greater than the radius of effect of a few kilotons; of towns and cities, say, a megaton. And a one-megaton weapon could erase the heart of a great city like Philadelphia, and kill instantly a third, a half, of its citizens. Once nuclear weapons come to be regarded as weapons that can be used, as opposed to instruments whose powers of destruction deter all thought of war, they cease to have whatever strategic meaning their possession implies. *

Since the post-war arms-race began, the world has without doubt become a more perilous place than it has ever been in human history. Why then does the

---

* If the NATO policy of 'flexible response' were regarded as a means of waging actual war, then the concept would be equivalent to a game of 'chicken' with nuclear weapons. The theatre nuclear weapons about which there is so much talk today—for example, cruise missiles and SS20s—are not the equivalent of the thousands of conventional bombs and shells that were expended against targets of opportunity and in the battles of the Second World War and of Vietnam. NATO's armoury of so-called tactical weapons has been for years authoritatively and publicly stated to number only 7,000, of which it is now said that 1,000 are to be withdrawn. Current discussions of Russian SS20s and American cruise missiles are in terms of a few hundreds—numbers which cannot be related to scenarios of field warfare.

nuclear arms-race continue? Why is it that the scientists at the top, men who had all relevant information at their disposal, have failed to get their views accepted? Is the answer that the chief advisers did not enjoy the confidence of their presidents, of the kind that Lysenko had with Stalin and Cherwell with Churchill? If Khrushchev rather than Stalin had been the head of the USSR when Lysenko was around, it is conceivable that he, the mystical and fraudulent plant-breeder, rather than his opponent Vavilov, an internationally-famed geneticist, would have to come to an untimely end in a labour camp. Had Churchill preferred Tizard's company to that of Cherwell, it is just possible that the area-bombing of German cities would not have been the preferred and dubious policy of RAF Bomber Command. But I doubt very much whether in the post-war period decisions which have spurred the nuclear arms-race would have been significantly different from what they have been had any of the top advisers concerned enjoyed a closer relationship than they did with the Presidents or Secretaries of Defense whom they served. The problem was certainly not one which involved personal relationships.

The normal run of political leader, whatever his ambitions, has inevitably been nurtured in an environment of politics. It is his business to appreciate what the public wants. He has to understand what is demanded in, for example, the provision of public services, whether they be schools or hospitals. He learns to take decisions within the limits of the resources at his disposal. And he can inspect the results—whether roads or power stations—with his own eyes. In the management of the national economy he can understand the call for lower taxes and the considerations which drive his budget chiefs or treasury ministers to propose this or that policy. Needless to say, he does all this within the constraints imposed by the political system at whose centre he stands.

But when it comes to the technicalities of the arms-race, he is on different territory, on territory where the experts rule. And when we move into the nuclear world, I would go further and submit that military chiefs, who by convention are the official advisers on national security, merely serve as a channel through which the men in the laboratories transmit their views. For it is the man in the laboratory—not the soldier or sailor or airman—who at the start proposes that for this or that arcane reason it would be useful to improve an old or to devise a new nuclear warhead; and if a new warhead, then a new missile; and, given a new missile, a new system within which it has to fit. It is he, the technician, not the commander in the field, who starts the process of formulating the so-called military need. It is he who has succeeded over the years in equating, and so confusing, nuclear destructive power with military strength, as though the former were the single and a sufficient condition of military success. The men in the nuclear weapons laboratories of both sides have succeeded in creating a world with an irrational foundation, on which a new set of political realities has in turn had to be built. They have become the alchemists of our times, working in secret ways which cannot be divulged, casting spells which embrace us all. They may never have been in a battle, they may never have experienced the devastation of war; but they know how to devise the means of destruction. And the more destructive power there is, so, one must assume they imagine, the greater the chance of military success.

None of this process constituted a mystery which the top presidential advisers failed to understand. Kistiakowsky, the scientist who was responsible for devising the implosion system for the first atom bombs, has published a record[24] of his days as President Eisenhower's Science Adviser, in which he tells how the President's policies were always frustrated by those who consistently 'exaggerated' the Soviet military threat. And he has no hesitation in declaring that any analysis of the predictions that have been made of the Soviet military threat over the past twenty years will show that they have always been far-fetched. York refers to a steady flow of 'phony intelligence' from a variety of sources, and writes that 'those of us who had all the facts in the matter and who knew there was no real basis for any of these claims [i.e. about Russian intentions and capacities] were hamstrung in any attempts we made to deal with them by the secrecy which always surrounds real intelligence information.' Herbert Scoville, who was in charge of scientific intelligence for the CIA during the sixties, makes the same point in a small book which was published in 1970 under the title *Missile Madness*.[25] So have others who were in the picture.

Why then has all the authoritative testimony on these matters from respected and highly informed scientists been set aside over the past two decades? Why, instead, have the nuclear bomb enthusiasts been heeded? 'The guilty men and organizations', writes York,[26] a self-declared ex-participant in the arms-race, 'are to be found at all levels of government and in all segments of society: Presidents, Presidential candidates; governors and mayors, members of Congress, civilian officials and military officers; business executives and labor leaders, famous scientists and run-of-the-mill engineers; writers and editorialists; and just plain folks.' Their motives, he tells us, are various, but 'nearly all such individuals,' he goes on to say,

> have had a deep long-term involvement in the arms race. They derive either their incomes, their profits, or their consultant fees from it. But much more important than money as a motivating force are the individuals' own psychic and spiritual needs; the majority of the key individual promoters of the arms race derive a very large part of their self-esteem from their participation in what they believe to be an essential—even a holy—cause. . . . They are inspired by ingenious and clever ideas, challenged by bold statements of real and imaginary military requirements, stimulated to match or exceed technological progress by the other side or even by a rival military service here at home, and victimized by rumors and phony intelligence. Some have been lured by the siren call of rapid advancement,

personal recognition, and unlimited opportunity, and some have been bought by promises of capital gains. Some have sought out
and even made up problems to fit the solution
they have spent much of their lives discovering and developing. A few have used the
arms race to achieve other, often hidden objectives.

If one were to leave out the matter of financial gain, I
imagine that the same words could equally be applied
to the Russians.

Donald Brennan, a mathematician who for a
period was President of the Hudson Institute, and who
had long involved himself in the discussion of strategic
matters, participated in the Congressional hearings on
the ABM system, and in the course of his testimony
made a most revealing statement. While it is conceivable that expenditure on ABMs could properly come
under Congressional scrutiny, such scrutiny, so he declared, did not apply to the technicalities of an ABM
system. As he put it,[27] 'The judgment about the best
means should be based on a complex of factors that
can scarcely be grasped whole by a full-time Secretary
of Defense. That a committee of the Congress could
meaningfully penetrate such a judgment seems to me
most unlikely.'

Brennan was in no doubt that it was the technician
who was paramount in decisions about nuclear weapons. And, while they well understand the way nuclear
illusions were and still are generated, chief scientific

advisers have proved to be no match for the laboratory technicians and the other participants in the nuclear arms-race.

Part of the reason for their failure is the fact that the weapons laboratories have a continuous existence, whereas presidents and prime ministers and military chiefs are both impermanent and concerned with a host of problems in addition to East-West relations and the nuclear arms-race. Over the past thirty years each of them has started his term of office from a different and higher nuclear plateau without any change in the political and strategic realities. *This is a critical fact which keeps being forgotten as the nuclear arms-race pursues its relentless course.*

Given the existence of nuclear weapons—and no one supposes that they are going to be swept away—the concept of mutual deterrence, based upon an appreciation of the enormous destructiveness of nuclear weapons, is valid and inescapable. But as the years pass there is something relevant to this proposition that we are inclined to forget. It is that whatever the number of nuclear weapons each side then possessed, a state of mutual deterrence was certainly already in existence by at least the late fifties and early sixties. Even at the worst moments of the cold war neither side was prepared to risk hostilities which would result in what was euphemistically called 'a level of unacceptable damage'. Cuba was a prime example of the reality of the concept of nuclear deterrence. I believe that there were other occasions when both sides were fearful of approaching the nuclear brink. It is the height of folly to lose sight of such practical demonstrations as we have already had of the reality of nuclear deterrence. Since the mid-fifties, the number of nuclear warheads on both sides has multiplied, let us say, fifty times—whatever the exact number does not matter—but the concept of deterrence has not altered. All that has changed is, first, that with every accretion to our respective arsenals, the level of so-called 'acceptable damage'—the essentially arbitrary and abstract concept which underlies mutual deterrence—has in effect been raised. And second, we are still encouraged to believe that a nuclear war could in fact be fought. The reification of the concept of so-called 'flexible response' on a European battlefield implies no real gap between conventional and nuclear arms.

The process of the nuclear arms-race clearly has no logic. In the early 1970s, when Henry Kissinger occupied high political office, he declared that no meaning could any longer be attached to the concept of 'nuclear superiority'; in his view, the threshold of nuclear armaments for both the Western and Eastern blocs was already well above what was needed to assure a state of mutual deterrence. Since then I have read that in his criticism of the Carter phase of the SALT II negotiations, he observed that what had been agreed in the treaty would allow the USSR to build up and modernise its nuclear armoury to a level which would threaten its 'equivalence' with that of the USA. I do not pretend to understand what he intended by this later statement. It is as though two already armed parties to a suicide pact were to start arguing as to who had the more lethal weapon, or whether the addition of a draught of cyanide would add assurance to the effects of a bullet through the brain or the heart.

When talking about the 'modernisation' of NATO's nuclear armoury, Kissinger is reported[28] as having said that the European allies of the United States should not keep asking the USA 'to multiply strategic assurances that we cannot possibly mean or if we do mean, we should not want to execute because if we execute we risk the destruction of civilization.' No stronger endorsement than this could ever be sought for the paradox enunciated by York and Wiesner in 1964[29]—that the continued growth of nuclear arsenals does not increase but decreases national security.*

---

* I know, of course, that Kissinger was one of those who not only favoured the continuation of R&D on, and the limited deployment of, an ABM system; but that he also supported the MIRV programme and argued for what is commonly called a counterforce strategy, instead of one based on the doctrine of 'assured destruction'[30]—that is to say, one based on the concept that mutual deterrence would persist so long as it was assumed that centres of population were to be treated as targets. And I also know that he has justified these views by declaring them to constitute a more humane policy than the one based on 'assured destruction'. In so far as discussions on strategy now seem to assume that the Russians share these views, and that were the state of deterrence to break down their nuclear offensive would begin with an assault on American fixed missile sites—with the USA striking at the corresponding military targets in the USSR —one could suppose that the policy that Kissinger eschews has become, at least implicitly, the prevailing doctrine. If I am correct in believing this, it is still inevitable that were military installations rather than cities to become the objectives of nuclear attack, millions, even tens of millions, of civilians would nonetheless be killed, whatever the proportion of missile sites, airfields, armament plants, ports, and so on that would be destroyed. Statements of the accuracy of missile

What he was also implicitly saying in Brussels was that while the Russians already have it in their power to eliminate at a stroke all the major cities of the NATO powers, and while the two European states which are nuclear powers already possess nuclear arsenals big enough to bring enormous destructive power to bear on the USSR, it was up to the European partners in NATO to go through a learning process which had already run its course in the United States. For the lesson to which Kissinger was pointing was that the two major powers have already learnt that nuclear war is no way to settle political differences; that if the battle is for the hearts and souls of men, there is no point in 'winning' one for the hearts of the dead. Individuals might well choose death rather than dishonour. But without invoking any moral principles, I hold that there

---

strikes are given in terms of the acronym, CEP (circular error probable), i.e. the radius of a circle within which fifty per cent of strikes would fall. People are inclined to forget about the other fifty per cent. Even if one were to assume that navigational and homing devices worked perfectly, the fifty per cent outside the magic circle would not necessarily be distributed according to Gaussian law. Moreover, whatever the accuracy with which they could be delivered, nuclear weapons still have an enormous area of effect relative to the precise 'military' targets at which the supposed counterforce strikes would be aimed. Lastly, were a nuclear exchange ever to be embarked upon, it seems inevitable that the side which felt it was losing would use other elements of its nuclear armoury against centres of population.

The entire concept of nuclear war, as opposed to deterrence, becomes a kind of Wonderland in the hands of civilian analysts who, unlike the chief scientific advisers who have been engaged in the debates, do not know at the technical level the *vis a tergo* in the process of elaborating nuclear warheads.

is no military sense in the scenario of a nuclear holocaust in which tens—hundreds—of millions on both sides would be sure to die. Moreover, I cannot see that this is a realistic option that is open to any democratically elected political leader—or one that could be exacted by any dictator—for a failure to win an armsrace for which no technical end could ever be envisaged.

It seems all but incredible that the battle which the Presidential Science Advisers have waged with those who participated technically in the race at operational levels below their own seems to have been a lost cause from the start. All the Presidential Science Advisers and the Directors of Defense Research and Engineering with whom I have discussed the problem recognise that once the threshold of mutual nuclear deterrence had been crossed, there was no technical sense in the further elaboration or multiplication of nuclear weapon systems. But this is not the point of view that has got across. Instead, their opponents knew how to respond to the mood of the country, how to capture the attention of the media, how to stir the hearts of generals. They have been adept at taking the short-term view and in creating the climate within which political chiefs have to operate. The longer term view of the top advisers— that the arms-race feeds itself, that there is no technical solution to the problem of defence against nuclear weapons—that view is too difficult to put across, strangely, I believe, not because it sounds soft and defeatist, but because it is too simple and too logical, and because the basic facts have become submerged in a sea of acronyms and numbers, a sea of MIRVs, of particle beams, of 'throw-weights', and so on. And the political chiefs whom the chief scientific advisers serve, and who are only in office for brief periods, inevitably find themselves in situations that leave little room for manoeuvre—situations characterised by an inertia and a resistance to change which is only to be expected when hundreds of thousands of the electors on whom they depend are making their livings doing things which were promoted years before by their political predecessors. It is the past which imbues the arms-race with its inner momentum.

I began by asking whether C. P. Snow had drawn conclusions of too general a kind from the story of the Cherwell-Tizard feud, and in particular of the danger of having chief scientific advisers isolated in the company of presidents and prime ministers. While not failing to appreciate his concern about the possible hazards of having a malign scientist in an isolated position at the summit of a political tree, I would be inclined to think that his fears were misplaced. The Tizard-Cherwell-Churchill saga was something *sui generis*. Postwar history, and particularly the story of the nuclear arms-race, has shown that even when, far from being isolated, chief scientific advisers arm themselves with the advice of colleagues as wise as those who over the years have served as members of PSAC, they can still fail to achieve what, given the positions of influence they occupy, C. P. Snow clearly feels they should have done.

We cannot, of course, disregard the reciprocal hostility, suspicion, and fears that have separated the Western and Eastern powers since at least the end of the Second World War. But basically the reason for the failure of the top scientific advisers to have any significant effect on the nuclear arms-race is that authority in the Western democracies has become too diffused, that the power of presidents and prime ministers—even of dictators—is far less absolute than is generally supposed by the people at whose head they stand. In my early days as a government adviser, a British civil servant of the old school, a man who had been the permanent head of two Departments of State, warned me that no bureaucrat, no official adviser, could be more effective than the minister whom he served. I did not quite appreciate what he meant at the time. Now I do. I do not doubt that those of our political leaders who have been involved over the years in the build-up of nuclear arsenals—perhaps the Russian leaders as well—were forced by political circumstances to take the decisions which they took, decisions which have not only made the future perilous for themselves, but which have encouraged other nations to follow their example, so still further endangering the peace of the world. They were driven to do as they did because they lacked the power to do otherwise, and consequently the power to delegate to their chief scientific advisers the authority which would have permitted them to impose their views on those of their subordinates by whom they had been ignored. On the other hand, from what has since happened, it seems clear that the chief scientific advisers by whom our political leaders were served were acutely aware that the failure to come to terms with the USSR would never be justified by whatever political prizes their masters sought to gain by succumbing to the pressures of those who wanted the nuclear arms-race to continue. Above all, the advisers recognised that there was no technical road to victory in an arms-race. Both sides were, and still are, bound to lose such a race. Defeat is indivisible in a war of nuclear weapons. Once a state of mutual deterrence had been reached, nuclear competition had nothing to contribute to the resolution of the political differences between West and East.

If scientific advisers cannot be more effective than those whom they advise, what then? No modern government could survive without their help because, as I have said, the problems with which they have to deal are largely the consequence of the exploitation of scientific knowledge. Scientific advisers—and scientific administrators—are therefore essential at all levels of government. Equally, however, the advisers cannot expect to disregard the political constraints which delimit the freedom of action of their masters. The story of the nuclear arms-race makes this only too plain. It is not isolation at the top that is the problem; it is the fact that no consensus can be expected among scientists who are involved in issues dominated by sectional vested interests, particularly those where the views of government scientists at lower levels are supported by powerful constituencies such as the military and certain sections of industry.

Obviously, when chief scientific advisers see their masters pursuing policies which they judge to be misguided, even when such policies reflect political pressures to which a president or prime minister may have had to succumb, they can go on trying to have them changed, or at least to save as much as they can from the wreckage. They have, of course, another option. There is nothing to stop chief scientific advisers from changing roles and from entering the race that ends in leadership and power, as opposed to spending their lives in the back rooms of politics. Men and women are not born with the acumen that is the dominant characteristic of the really able politician, any more than statesmanship and political vision necessarily derive from electoral and parliamentary success. If those who strive to become political leaders can learn from the experience they gain as politicians, surely the trained scientist—or at least some trained scientists—could do the same? But if they were to choose this course, they would then have to be ready to accept all the frustrations that go with such office, and be ready to make all the compromises that are associated with the exercise of power in a democracy.

In the long run, I believe, another option will present itself. It was Francis Bacon[31] who wrote that 'human knowledge and human power do really meet in one; and it is from ignorance of causes that operation fails.' His dreams of a rational society based on 'advanced science and technique' were, of course, spelt out long before the start of the industrial revolution. For the kind of society in which we now live to become rational in Francis Bacon's sense, we need far more open and informed public discussion of the immediate 'causes' that have turned today's advanced industrial societies into the armed camps which they now are.

These 'causes' are only remotely related to those which underlie the essential political and economic problems that will have to be solved in the decades ahead, even in the centuries ahead, if our world is to become sufficiently peaceful to assure the continuity of our species. As York and Kistiakowsky have emphasised, to expose these problems to public gaze we need far less of the secrecy that is the environment in which the nuclear arms-race pursues its irrational course.

We need to take advantage of the fact that the context of public opinion within which major issues of policy have to be decided is already, even if slowly, changing; that it is moving in a more open and liberal direction. Our political leaders are handicapped in reaching wise decisions in the field on which I have focused when unnecessary secrecy—that is to say, secrecy which does not prejudice national security—is able to inhibit proper discussion among the informed. Unfortunately, there are no open 'science courts' to serve as forums for debate on the big issues with which chief scientific advisers have to deal. But the problems of the nuclear arms-race will never be resolved except through the encouragement of open discussion of matters where the rules of official secrecy are exploited, not because of the need for security, but to promote partisan policies; when, in Gunnar Myrdal's words, scientific knowledge is steered for a purpose. That is what needs to be changed. The majority of countries are committed to a policy of non-proliferation, and no one would therefore want information spread about the technology of nuclear weapons. But the aims of the Non-Proliferation Treaty would only be furthered if there were a clearer public understanding about the effects of nuclear weapons. And how can an informed public be expected to understand the arguments about SALT II and the CTB if they cannot participate because they are denied access to facts which, if one takes the trouble, one can usually find in the public domain because of 'leaks'?

I sometimes like to play the scenario backwards and ask myself what the world would have been like if, in the early sixties, the views of the Killians, the Wiesners, the Kistiakowskys, and the Yorks had prevailed, rather that those that proved dominant and which were born out of a matrix stirred by diverse political pressures. I do not doubt that there would have been more than enough major issues for the chief advisers to deal with and which would have defied easy solution, or perhaps any solution at all: for example, agreeing on the best energy policy, or how to control genetic engineering or population growth, or how to provide technological aid to Third World countries. These may not be so urgent, but they are far more important issues than the arms-race which now consumes so much of the scarcest of our national resources—informed experience and wise judgment.

REFERENCES

1. Snow, C. P., 1961, *Science and Government* (Godkin Lectures, Harvard) London: Oxford University Press.
2. Snow, C. P., 1959, *The Two Cultures and the Scientific*

Revolution (Rede Lectures), London: Cambridge University Press.

3. Snow, C. P., 1962, *A Postscript to Science and Government*, London: Oxford University Press.

4. Price, Don K., 1954, *Government and Science*, New York: New York University Press.

5. Wiesner, J. B., 1965, *Where Science and Politics Meet*, New York: McGraw-Hill.

6. Watson-Watt, R., 1948, *Advancement of Science*, 4, 320.

7. Zuckerman, Solly, 1978, *From Apes to Warlords*, London: Hamish Hamilton.

8. Turnbull, H. W. (ed.), 1961, *The Correspondence of Isaac Newton*, 3, 364.

9. 'Lavoisier', *Encyclopaedia Britannica* (11 ed), 1911.

10. Valéry, P., 1936, 'La Politique de l'Esprit', *Variété*, 3.

11. Baldwin, S., 1931, Election speech at the Queen's Hall, Manchester, 17 March.

12. Churchill, W. S., 1947, *Hansard, House of Commons*, 444 Cols 206–7.

13. *Eisenhower, D. D., 1961, Public Papers of the President, 1960–1961,* p. 1038. Washington D.C.: US Government Printing Office.

14. Nelkin, D., 1978, *Technological Decisions and Democracy*, London: Saga.

15. Killian, J. R. Jr, 1977, *Sputnik, Scientists, and Eisenhower*, Cambridge, Mass: MIT Press.

16. Kistiakowsky, G. B., 1976, *A Scientist at the White House*, Cambridge, Mass: Harvard University Press; and 1979, 'False alarm: The story behind SALT II', *New York Review of Books*, 22 March, pp. 33–38.

17. York, H. F., 1970, *Race to Oblivion*, New York: Simon & Schuster.

18. *Long-term Worldwide Effects of Multiple Nuclear-Weapons Detonations*, Washington DC: National Academy of Sciences, 1975; *Economic and Social Consequences of Nuclear Attacks on the United States*, Washington DC: US Government Printing Office, 1979; US Congress Of-

fice of Technology Assessment, 1979, *The Effects of Nuclear War*, Washington D.C.: US Arms Control and Disarmament Agency, 1979, *The Effects of Nuclear War*.

19. United Nations, 1968, *Effects of the Possible Use of Nuclear Weapons . . .* , New York: United Nations; and Zuckerman, Sir Solly, 1966, 'Facts and Reason in a Nuclear Age', *Scientists and War*, London: Hamish Hamilton.

20. Wiesner, J. B., and H. F. York, 1964, 'National Security and the Nuclear Test Ban', *Scientific American*, 211(4), 27.

21. See note 17.

22. *Defence, Outline of Future Policy*, London: HMSO (Cmnd 124), 1957.

23. Zuckerman, S., 1962, 'Judgment and Control in Modern Warfare', *Foreign Affairs*, 40(2), 196–212.

24. See note 16.

25. Scoville, H., and R. Osborn, 1970, *Missile Madness*, Boston: Houghton Mifflin.

26. See note 17.

27. See note 17.

28. Jobert, M., 1979, *International Herald Tribune* (Paris ed), 22 October.

29. See note 20.

30. Kissinger, H., 1979, *White House Years*, Boston: Little, Brown.

31. Bacon, Francis, 1960, 'The Great Instauration: Preface', *The New Organon and Related Writings*, ed. F. H. Anderson, New York: Liberal Arts.

Glossary

ABM	Anti-ballistic missile defence
ACARD	(British) Advisory Council for Applied Research and Development
ACSP	(British) Advisory Council on Scientific Policy
BMD	Ballistic missile defence
CEP	Circular error probable. The radius of a circle whose centre is the aiming point and within which 50% of strikes would be expected to fall
CERN	Centre Européen pour la Recherche Nucléaire
Cruise	Low-flying pilotless aircraft of medium or long range
DRPC	(British) Defence Research Policy Committee
ICBM	Inter-continental ballistic missile
IRBM	Intermediate-range ballistic missile
MIRV	Multiple independently-targetable re-entry vehicle fitted to a ballistic missile
MX	US mobile inter-continental ballistic missile
NASA	(US) National Aeronautics and Space Administration
NORAD	North American Aerospace Defense Command

NSF	(US) National Science Foundation
OMB	(US) Office of Management and Budget
OST	(US) Office of Science and Technology
OSTP	(US) Office of Science and Technology Policy
Pershing II	US medium-range ballistic missile
Polaris	US submarine-launched ballistic missile
SAC	(US) Strategic Air Command
SDI	Strategic Defense Initiative
SLBM	Submarine-launched ballistic missile
SS4, SS5	Soviet medium-range ballistic missiles
SS18	Soviet inter-continental ballistic missile
SS20	Soviet mobile intermediate-range ballistic missile
Throw weight	The total weight of the last stage carried by a ballistic missile
Trident	US submarine-launched ballistic missile
U2	US reconnaissance aircraft

INDEX

ABOUT THE AUTHOR

Solly Zuckerman began researching the biological effects of bomb blast for the British government at the start of World War II. He was then a strategic air planner in the Mediterranean and Normandy campaigns. After the war, he served on numerous councils and committees and was deputy chairman of the advisory council on scientific policy. From 1960 to 1966 he was chief scientific advisor to the British Ministry of Defense, and from 1966 to 1971, he was chief scientific advisor to the British government. When he retired, he was made a life peer. He is the author of numerous scientific works and of *From Apes to Warlords*, *Nuclear Illusion and Reality* (also available from Vintage), *Scientists and War*, and *Beyond the Ivory Tower*. Lord Zuckerman lives in England.